The Actor's Field Guide

Acting Notes on the Run

ED HOOKS

BACK STAGE BOOKS
An imprint of Watson-Guptill Publications / New York

Senior Editor: Mark Glubke
Editor: Michelle Bredeson
Cover designed by Eric J. Olson
Interior designed by Cheryl Viker
Production Manager: Ellen Greene

Published in 2004 by Back Stage Books,
an imprint of Watson-Guptill Publications,
a division of VNU Business Media, Inc.,
770 Broadway, NY 10003
www.watsonguptill.com

Library of Congress Cataloging-in-Publication Data

Hooks, Ed.
  The actor's field guide : acting notes on the run / Ed Hooks.
     p. cm.
Includes bibliographical references and index.
 ISBN 0-8230-0115-6
 1. Acting. I. Title.
 PN2061.H643 2004
 792.02'8—dc22
                                           2003024539

Manufactured in U.S.A.

First printing, 2004

1 2 3 4 5 6 7 8 9 / 12 11 10 09 08 07 06 05 04

I would like to dedicate this book to all who approach acting with respect as an art form.

Actors are shamans.

Acknowledgments

A tall and slender man named Richard Casey, teaching at the American Academy of Dramatic Arts in New York, taught me in 1970 what it means to play an action. He made up an exercise in which I was to pretend to be asleep in a cabin in Alaska and he was pretending to be a polar bear. My instructions were to get my shoes and escape once the bear came inside my shack. Three times the bear caught and ate me as I tried to get my shoes on. The fourth time, I picked up the shoes and ran barefoot out into the snow. "Yes! That's it, love!" he exclaimed with delight. The action was to escape, not to put on the shoes. It was an invaluable bit of theatrical wisdom. To this day, I cite his lesson to me in my own workshops for the benefit of a new generation of actors. I will always be grateful to him.

The Actor's Field Guide is full to the brim with lessons taken directly from my acting classes, and I must thank my students for their good humor and professionalism. Many a time I have stopped mid-critique to jot down a salient point that would find its way into this book. In fact, it was one of my Chicago students, Kathy Corday, who first suggested to me the title for the book. And it was another of my students, Baird Tinkey, who sent me an e-mail bemoaning the fact that he had lost his class notes. He said, "You know, those notes would have made a good book." My effort to respond to him was the seed from which the field guide has grown.

Thanks to Mark Glubke, senior editor at Back Stage Books, for his faith in this project and to Michelle Bredeson, my primary editor on the book. Both of these artists have earned a standing ovation.

Intelligentsia Coffee on Broadway in the Lakeview neighborhood of Chicago makes Italian-caliber coffee and has generously allowed me to take up table space for the writing of much of this book. I'd like another double non-fat latte, please. And thanks.

It is not easy to live with someone who is writing a book. After four previous books, my wife, Cally, and daughter, Dagny, have become Grand Masters in the patience department. Hugs to you both.

Contents

How to Use This Guide

The Actor's Field Guide is to an actor what a field guide to exotic birds is to a birdwatcher—an easy-to-use, information-packed reference that you can use on the go. In addition to offering practical advice, *The Actor's Field Guide* is intended to be quick and easy to use. You should, for example, be able to sit in a coffee shop or in the parking lot outside the audition studio and browse just a couple of pages for some pointers that will help you focus and perform better under pressure of audition.

Let's say you're rehearsing a funny play, but it doesn't seem very funny. You could use a little extra input about how to play comedy, a fresh perspective. Look up "comedy" in the index. Or maybe you want broader input on the rehearsal process itself? Try simply looking up "rehearsal." Got a scene in which you must cry and you're not sure how to go about it? Look up "crying."

Each chapter opens with an introductory essay that you don't have to read if you don't want to. If you have the time and want to read it, then great! The introductory essay will put the field notes into a bit more perspective, but the field notes are self-explanatory and should therefore be able to stand alone. Even if you are a beginning actor, the notes should make sense to you.

I have also included occasional boxed essays that expand on some of the trickier aspects of the actor's craft. These will even further illuminate the field notes and provide you with more to consider about the art and craft of acting. It is not, however, essential that you read the boxed notes in order to understand the field notes.

In short, if I have written this book correctly and with sufficient conciseness, you should be able to use it in short doses or big, according to your needs and preferences. It should function as a quick reference as well as provide fodder for deeper study. Each chapter should stand alone, each field note should stand alone but, if you want to really dig into the subjects, you have that option.

THE STYLE OF THE FIELD NOTES

The field notes in this book are real-world. They are lifted primarily from my professional acting classes and coaching sessions. Sometimes the notes will be blunt. On occasion they may even be a little off-color. That is because, though they may be occasionally thrilling, acting classes are not always neat and pretty. The field notes are written, for better or worse, in my voice and in the heat of the moment. I have elected not to edit them very much because I think you will get the most from them that way. Sometimes, tone conveys more meaning than the words themselves. I intend that this book be the opposite of literary.

Professional acting classes, regardless of the technique or approach being taught, take place in a very unique environment, with actors putting themselves on the line emotionally and personally in front of their peers in order to hone their skill in an elusive art. There are times when a class moves smoothly and other times when communication all but breaks down between coach and actor. I, like most teachers, will generally do whatever I must do in order to make a point. At times, it is only necessary to quietly point out a principle. At other times, it is necessary to become emphatic, to be blunt or to make jokes. A major component of any successful acting class is two-way trust. Given that the actor is exposing herself emotionally, she must be certain that the teacher will be constructive and non-exploitative. And a teacher must trust that his students share the same high standards as he so that everybody is marching to the same drummer.

Audition

Professional acting is a far different and more stressful proposition than what happens at most community theaters. The moment an actor says to the world, "Pay me to act," a whole different standard kicks in. If you want to be paid to act, you have to know how to give a competitive and compelling audition. If directors and producers are expected to write you a check for acting, they want to see the goods. The awful bottom line is that if your auditions are weak, you will not get many opportunities to do any actual acting. And you won't get paid.

There are the rare exceptions of course, but I advise you not to count on being one of them. A couple of directors I know laugh now about not casting Robert De Niro in his early days because they said he was a god-awful auditioner. And I recall directing a play in Hollywood for which I spent almost two hours in a private audition with a well-known movie actor who had been submitted for the lead role. I wanted to cast him because his celebrity alone would have helped sell tickets. I tried and tried to see the performance in him, but I couldn't see it. The man simply could not audition, and so I didn't cast him. I have never regretted it even though the light of his celebrity shines even brighter today than it did back then.

As a general rule, if they don't see magic in your audition, they'll thank you for coming and then proceed to the next actor. Rejection comes with an acting career the way trees come with woods. You will lose far more jobs than you will win, and the decisions of casting directors and producers will often make no sense at all to you. In spite of these poor odds, whenever you go to an audition you must walk in the door feeling that you deserve to be cast and should be cast. Actors who work a lot tend to be very strong in audition. They are not subservient to the auditors, and they take the lead in the audition itself. Their implied message is, "Thanks for having me in. Now sit back and let me show you how this thing will go if you use me." If you approach an audition doubtfully, the odds against you become even more staggering. Success and failure tend to be self-fulfilling prophesies.

THE RIGHT AUDITION FOR THE MEDIUM

It is true, to paraphrase Gertrude Stein, that an audition is an audition is an audition. In all auditions actors present their wares to one or more decision-making auditors. Whether the audition requires reading from scripts or presenting monologues or improvising, the actor still struts his stuff with the hope that he will be selected for the role. But it is equally true that all auditions are *not* the same. You don't present the same kind of audition for a commercial that you do for a stage play or for a film or for a TV show.

A stage audition is sort of like a display at the racetrack. The director wants to see your form and style and humor and intelligence as much as she wants to see a dead-on rendition of the character. When you audition for a stage play, you can make acting choices that are wildly wrong for the role and still get cast. That's because the director knows there will be rehearsal. She will cut you a lot of slack on interpretation if she sees potential and strength.

An audition for a film or a TV show is different. Unless the project you are reading for is a sitcom or a soap opera, you are not likely to get much, if any, rehearsal once you are cast. Rehearsal on a standard movie consists of running over things while the cameras are being set up. Therefore, in auditions for movies and TV shows, they want to see the performance. They want to see what you plan to do on the set. You can make strong acting choices, but you can't indulge in the sort of wildness that you can in a stage audition. I once presented Lucky's speech from *Waiting for Godot* verbatim backward at an audition for a Broadway play. I learned it last word first, next-to-last word second, and so on. Yes, it was showboating, but it got me into callbacks. If I had done a thing like that on a film or TV audition, it probably would have earned me an automatic rejection because it would have scared the director.

An audition for a television commercial is more about personality projection than anything else. Anybody, even nonactors, can do commercials. Mainly, you have to have a winning personality and come across as someone the producers want to spend a day with. Especially today, when over half of all commercials do not involve dialogue, the ability to sell yourself is more critical than selling the product. The implied message in a commercial is, "If I use this product, I will be like the person in the commercial."

FIELD NOTES

FIRST IMPRESSIONS

★ Approach an audition as if you already have the job and are there for a rehearsal.

★ The actor should *lead* in an audition. Casting decisions are often made within seconds of when you enter the room, even before you get a chance to read or present a monologue. Enter with confidence and welcoming benevolence, as if you are greeting the auditors in your own living room at home. When you get to the point in the entertainment business where you are auditioning mostly for jobs that pay money, you will discover that just about all of your competition is wonderfully talented. It's like competing against Tiger Woods every time you step up to the tee. At this level, success is often measured in small increments. A winning audition might depend on whoever appears most confident today for instance. If you can walk into the audition room and cause them to relax and look forward to what you are going to do, you have won half the battle before you begin.

★ At stage auditions, there is frequently a chair or stool set center stage for the use of the auditioning actors. If you are going to use it, move it before you begin, even if only a few inches one way or the other. Doing so sends a subtle message to the auditors that you are in charge and are taking a leadership position.

> In the theater, *stage right* and *stage left* are from the actor's perspective as she stands on stage facing the audience. *Downstage* is the area of the stage closest to the audience, and *upstage* is against the back wall.

★ Unless you are auditioning in front of a video camera, feel free to move around the room or stage. If there is any way you can avoid it, don't stand smack in front of the auditors. Stand off-center or move farther away from them, upstage left or upstage right. Actor after actor after actor has come into the audition room and stood in the same spot. Even before you open your mouth and utter the first line of dialogue, you will make a strong impression if you simply stand in a different place than where all the other actors have stood.

CASTING: A FLOW CHART

If you are up for a role that pays money, your first audition is generally going to be with a casting director. After that, you move upward by auditioning for the actual decision makers. Who the decision makers are depends on the medium. Final casting decisions for commercials are made by a committee consisting of ad agency execs, the client, and the director. For movie roles, though you may be auditioning in the room with writers and producers, the director usually is the one to make final decisions. For television shows, your auditors will likely include producers, writers, and the director, with the writers and producers typically carrying the most weight. On-going TV shows usually employ staff writers and producers while the directors come and go. If you are auditioning for a continuing role in a new TV series, you may also have to get final approval from network executives even though you have already been selected by the show's creative team.

PREPARATION

★ If you are going to do relaxation exercises, don't do them in the audition room. Do them in the hall where nobody can see you.

★ When you began your monologue a few minutes ago, you first turned your back on us and prepared. We sat here looking at your backside. As lovely as that view may be, starting out with your back to us sets the tone for a weak presentation. Enter the room, introduce yourself, tell the auditors what you will be doing, and then begin. You can take a brief moment at the top, but don't turn your back or look down at the floor. Look at your imaginary scene partner instead.

★ Performance anxiety is self-fulfilling. If you are worried about forgetting your lines, you are more likely to forget them. The correction to this is to play your action fully. Commit to the circumstances of the play. What does your character want or need in the scene? What do you want or need from your scene partner?

★ When rehearsing your monologue before an audition, do not try to "freeze" the reading!

★ Five minutes before you go into the audition room you will be overcome with the worst urge to urinate you have ever had in your life. Go ahead, but be quick about it and don't linger in front of the mirror. You already look good and fretting over your image will make you more nervous. Remember to wash your hands.

★ "Pull your hair back. I can't see your face."

WHAT TO BRING TO THE AUDITION

★ Always bring a headshot and resume, even if you think your agent already sent them over.

★ It's a good idea to bring breath freshener because auditions tend to be stressful, and stress can cause bad breath. Of course if you are a smoker, the breath freshener is even more essential. You don't want anybody in the audition room to think you smell like a Camel.

WHAT TO WEAR

★ Hmmmm...those are lovely and sexy leather pants, dear, but notice how they restrict your movement when you try to sit on the floor? Wear clothes that allow you to move.

★ What you wear affects how you feel and how you act. You're wearing a turtleneck sweater that completely covers the trunk of your body. In a way, you are hiding behind the sweater as if it were made of steel. Wear a loose-fitting open-neck shirt that exposes your throat and you will be amazed at how much more vulnerable you feel. If you feel more vulnerable, you will be more in touch with your emotions and you will be more accessible to the moment.

★ Don't wear jeans to auditions if you are over nineteen years old. Jeans tend to be associated more with young people than adults. You will appear more upscale and mature if you wear chinos or cords or a loose skirt.

★ I suggest you not wear really short skirts to stage auditions because it is always possible that you will be asked to do an improvisation or work on the floor. You want to be able to move around the stage, so wear something that is attractive but doesn't constrict your movement. Auditions for movies, commercials, and TV shows are usually conducted in a more confined space, like an office, so comfortable clothes are less of a priority.

★ It is totally up to you if you want to dress like the character for which you are auditioning. Marlon Brando reportedly stuffed cotton balls in his cheeks when he auditioned for the movie *The Godfather*. Some actors love to costume themselves for auditions, and I say good for them. Me personally? I sort of dress in the general direction of the character, but I don't micro-manage. If I'm auditioning for the role of a doctor, I'll wear a nice shirt and slacks but I will stop short of putting a stethoscope around my neck. There is something about over-costuming that bothers me. It feels somehow a bit too subservient. But that's just me. Like I say, many successful actors disagree with me about this. Pick your poison.

★ If you perspire a lot, don't wear clothes that show perspiration stains. Sweating may be a sign of pure exertion and exhilaration, but it could be misconstrued as pure nerves.

★ Avoid wearing bright and busy clothes, especially when you go to a commercial audition. Stick with muted colors like earth tones and pastels. No paisleys, no written messages on shirts. You want the auditors to be looking at your face, and loud or revealing clothing will upstage it.

CONFIDENCE

★ Visualize success. Before you enter the audition room, imagine yourself winning the part. Olympic athletes use this technique all the time, and you can too. See your success in your mind's eye, and then go do it.

★ Confidence manifests itself in a feeling of relaxation; relaxation manifests itself in a feeling of weight. When you are confident, you feel more centered, more connected to the earth. You literally feel "grounded." Anxiety is a high and heady thing. Notice how Woody Allen's energy, or power center, is mostly above his shoulders. In general, the higher your power center, the more anxious you will feel.

★ The avoidance of failure is not the same thing as the pursuit of success. Actors are too often perfectionists. They want to get it "right." The problem is that acting is never "right." It is pure process and will vary each time you do it. If you have a vision of perfection in your brain and then try not to screw that up, you are avoiding a negative. In other words you are trying to avoid failure. If you try, you'll make yourself nervous. Always pursue something positive in an audition. This does not mean to make your auditions uniformly cheerful or to act like Pollyanna. It means to pursue a positive outcome.

★ Every one of your sentences ends with an upward inflection, did you know that? This is known as "up talking." It is a modern politically correct way of checking with people around you to see if they would be willing to take a moment to consider your opinion. Assert yourself! Stop asking for permission to exist. Your opinions matter!

★ Success and failure are self-fulfilling prophesies.

DEALING WITH NERVES

★ You can't relax by ordering yourself to relax. When you tell yourself to relax, you have to think about how tense you are, which will just make you more tense. The best way to solve problems of tension is to redirect your thinking to the circumstances of the scene. If you are fully playing your actions, your tension will fade.

★ Regardless of how nervous you may feel, breathe deeply. Focus your mind. Keep your sense of humor and maintain a light touch. It is, after all, only an acting role. You are not responsible for finding a cure for cancer!

★ Tension is enemy number one for actors in audition. It blocks emotion and deflates your sense of humor. What you want to achieve is a kind of excitement instead of tension. Think of football players when they are getting ready to start the Super Bowl. They are awash with energy, but they have confidence. If they do not have confidence, the energy will become negative, turning into tension. Actors are similar to athletes in this regard. You are more likely to hurt yourself if you are tight and tense than if you are loose and excited.

★ Avoid sitting in the "toilet" position on that chair. Notice that when you lean forward that way, with your forearms resting on your thighs, your chest is pointed toward the floor? I know you're nervous and trying to protect yourself by sitting that way, but you're throwing your power into the floor. Sit up!

★ Actors get embarrassed when they experience fear and tension. For some reason, they think they should be immune to these basic human feelings. The truth is that fear and tension come with the territory. Auditions themselves are anxiety provoking and, if you are fortunate enough to be cast, you may be the kind of actor who wants to throw up right before an entrance. I read once that an actor's heartbeat and blood pressure as the curtain rises is roughly equivalent to that of an Air Force test pilot in full flight.

★ When I watch your monologue, I see a nervous actor. You're shifting from foot to foot, continually jamming your hand into your left pants pocket, and your eyes are darting around the room. If I could turn off the visuals and just listen to you, however, I would hear the words of a confident business tycoon. In other words, there is a divide between what you are doing and what you are saying. If you behaved like this in an actual audition, you'd probably lose the job because what the eye sees counts for more than what the ear hears.

★ Do you realize that you're holding your arms tightly down by your sides? Your tension is preventing you from gesturing. Watch me as I'm talking with you. I gesture, don't I? Watch people around you in the world. They gesture! And because the human sense of sight is so powerful, if you don't gesture when it seems reasonable that you would, the auditors will feel ill at ease.

★ Renowned acting teacher Michael Chekhov had the right approach to dealing with tension. Instead of instructing actors to relax, he would tell them to move "with ease."

SELECTING AUDITION MATERIAL

★ Directors and casting directors for stage plays often ask the actor to first present one or two monologues. After this, they move on to reading with the actor from the actual script or perhaps to some kind of improvisation. Monologues give them a chance to see you putting your best foot forward. They presume you have carefully selected the material to dynamically display your talent and that you have worked it up to performance level. In other words, when they look at your monologues, they are thinking this is probably as good as you are going to get. This is why the monologues you present are especially important. They are frequently the front gate you must open in order to go further into the audition process.

★ Having a selection of compelling monologues is as important as having a winning headshot. You need at least four: contemporary comedy and drama, and classical comedy and drama. Usually, people think of classical as Shakespeare. I have known actors who are always ready with as many as sixteen or eighteen monologues, but most actors have six or eight. With that many, you can mix and match depending on the type of audition you are facing. If, for instance, you are auditioning for a season of repertory, it is possible they will present a play by Shakespeare or Molière. In that case, you really should have classical monologues at the ready. If you are auditioning for a single play, you will probably do best with contemporary selections.

★ My observation from watching auditions over the years is that most actors would prefer to present dramatic monologues rather than comedy. For this reason, you will be at a competitive advantage if you have really strong comic material in your quiver. At stage auditions, physical comedy is generally stronger than a monologue in which you stand in a single spot. A good comic monologue should not be confused with a stand-up comedy routine. You can use those stationary comic monologues better if you are auditioning on videotape, say in an agent's office. Stage auditions should ideally be more physically dynamic.

★ Special advice for women: When selecting monologue material from Shakespeare's plays, consider doing men's roles. I have seen a couple of jaw-dropping wonderful female Mark Anthonys *(Julius Caesar)* and Iagos *(Othello)* for instance. When you portray male roles it immediately broadcasts to the auditors that you are your own person. It catches their attention, almost always in a positive way.

★ You'd make a marvelous Trinculo in *The Tempest,* Mary. Don't worry that the role was written for a man. All of Shakespeare's roles were written for men, because his theater employed no actresses. Since men played all of Shakespeare's female characters, there are simply not as many wonderful female roles to choose from, especially in the thirty- to forty-five-year-old age range. We can't be concerned with that anymore. If the role speaks to you and you think you can have fun with it, then do it.

★ When selecting classical comedy material, women might want to look at Molière in addition to Shakespeare. Molière came along about a hundred years after Shakespeare and wrote wonderful, strong, lusty, bright, and witty women. The prime female comedy roles in Shakespeare are so well known and are presented so often in audition that you might be at a competitive advantage if you tap Molière. In particular, look for Richard Wilbur's translations of Molière. They are like a china bell.

PRESENTING YOUR MONOLOGUE

★ Don't take that little step forward on the first line of your monologue. Hold still. You'll come across stronger.

★ When presenting a monologue at a stage audition, you may be tempted to speak directly to the auditors. This approach may not always work. When I was doing most of my early auditioning in New York, I used to make frequent eye contact with auditors and I never received a single complaint. Same thing in Los Angeles. Then I auditioned in San Francisco, and the casting directors balked. Same thing in Chicago. The bottom line is that, since I cannot tell you with 100 percent certainty that it is okay to direct your monologue to an auditor, it is probably the most prudent choice for you to speak to an imaginary scene partner. Either that or you could try saying to the auditor, just prior to your presentation, "I would like to direct this monologue to you. Would that be okay?" Be prepared for a "no" answer and hope for a "yes."

★ Why do you look at the floor the moment before you begin your monologue? What's down there? Don't tell me. I know what you're doing. You're thinking about your lines. The problem is that it looks like a preparation of some kind, and you are already on stage in front of the auditors. That kind of work should be done off stage. You ought now to be looking at the person you're talking to.

★ When you are presenting a monologue, be very specific about where your imaginary scene partner is on stage. Get the eye level right. You look like you're talking to a person a foot shorter than you, and it's a bit distracting.

★ When talking to imaginary scene partners in monologues or in commercials, I have always gotten a lot of mileage out of directing my speech to someone who is very understanding but mildly skeptical of everything I say.

★ Actors often make a common mistake when presenting monologues. You just know when they step up there and open their mouths that they are about to do a big monologue. In life, we don't set out to do big monologues. We set out to make a point, and then we build on the point once the person we're talking to grasps it. Or sometimes we'll make a point and then, upon our own reflection, continue with an amplification of that point. What I'm saying is that you don't want to get up on stage at an audition and subliminally broadcast to everybody in the room that this is going to be a long speech. Keep them guessing! A monologue can and should be broken down into communicative hierarchical segments.

★ Try making the first line of your monologue the response to an unspoken line. Acting is reacting. If the first line of your monologue appears to be a reaction to something, it will ring a bit more true than if you just open your mouth and start talking. A monologue is really a duologue. The person you are talking to is not really on the stage with you, but you should still be reactive to her.

★ You're launching into your monologue too quickly. I'm not expecting you to do one of those Ed Norton false-start hand-gesturing routines from the old *Honeymooners* sitcom, but I do expect you to focus and center yourself before you start talking. Your anxiety is getting the best of you. It is the equivalent of a boxer walking into the center of the ring and just flailing away. That would be a very good way to get your silly self knocked out. Take a breath. Focus. Then begin.

★ In general, I think it is stronger for the auditioning actor to stand rather than sit while presenting a monologue. There are several reasons for this. First, if you stand, the auditors can see your whole body. Second, nervous and self-doubting actors tend to hang on to furniture. If you come into the audition room and immediately sit on that chair center stage, the auditors will have to decide if they are looking at a nervous actor or one who really needs to sit in order for the monologue to work. Unless you absolutely must sit, your best choice is to stand.

CASTING DIRECTORS

Casting directors are vitally important in the industry, but their job title is something of a misnomer. The fact is that the casting director rarely makes the final decision about who gets cast and who does not. A casting director's job is to function as a sort of creative filter through which actors must pass en route to auditions in front of the final decision makers. Since there are many more actors seeking work than there are jobs, a talented casting director can bring order and grace to what can be an otherwise unwieldy process. She will sort through photos and resumes and pre-screen actors to decide who are the strongest and most appropriate candidates for the roles. If she does not already know the actor's work, she may audition him privately before deciding whether to take him to the producers and director. In the case of commercials, she or her assistant will likely videotape the first audition for later replay and consideration by an assembled group of decision makers, including the producers, director, copywriter, account executives, and, of course, the client.

★ I don't want to sound too mystical, but imagine that you have an aura around you. Okay? Concentrate on your aura for a moment. Create a visual image of it in your mind. Notice that your aura extends maybe a foot away from your body? Now, as you present your monologue, I want you to project that aura out so that it envelops the entire room. Project your entire self, not just your voice!

READING FROM THE SCRIPT

★ When you are auditioning for a play or movie, script in hand, reading with a casting director or stage manager, keep your head up when she is reading the other character's lines. Then glance back down to the script to get your next line. Let me put this another way. When the stage manager or casting director is reading the other character's lines, you ought not be reading along with her. Watch the other person reading with you, listen to what she says, and react. If you don't do it this way, it will appear that you are only acting "on the line." In other words, don't stop acting when the other person is reading.

★ To the extent that you can, use the reality of the casting director in an audition. In this instance, I am reading with you, but I am obviously not a sixty-year-old woman, as it says in the script. When you look at me, you're going to see a male. Still, you should try to connect with me personally when you read your lines that are, in the story, spoken to the middle-aged woman. When you look at me, don't waste time trying to hallucinate me into an old woman. Deal with me.

★ At most television and movie auditions, you will read with a casting director while the actual decision makers watch. At auditions for commercials, you will be paired with another actor if the script calls for dialogue.

★ Don't touch the casting director. You can shake hands with him when you enter the room but, after that, don't touch him. If you are reading for a scene in which your character might, for example, restrain the other character by grabbing her arm, do not grab the casting director's arm. If your scene is with a child and you have the impulse to tussle his hair, don't tussle the casting director's hair. If you have even a non-romantic kiss in a scene, do not kiss the casting director.

CALLBACK STRATEGIES

★ A callback audition typically involves going through the same paces you went through at the first audition, but it is a good strategy not to try to duplicate your first audition exactly. Keep your performance fresh! If you attempt to do at a callback precisely what you did at the first audition, your acting will appear stale and un-spontaneous. You will also be more likely to get nervous. Remember, acting happens in the present moment. Your first audition took place in a former present moment; the callback takes place in a new present moment. If the director at a callback says, "Just do what you did last time," don't do it. Say the same words and play the same actions, but motivate the entire thing as if you have never done it before.

> The field of actors competing for a role is narrowed at the first audition. Any audition after that is referred to as a *callback*. Callback auditions happen in all media. There may in fact be more than one callback for a major role in a TV show, Broadway play, movie, or important advertising campaign.

COMMERCIALS

★ When you go to an audition for a commercial, look around the waiting room to see if there is a storyboard. A storyboard is a black-and-white hand-drawn panel cartoon rendering of what the ad agency people are looking to shoot. It can be helpful in giving you a feel for the spot's dynamic.

★ Taped commercial auditions present special considerations for the actor, particularly if you are on camera with another actor. You have to "cheat" toward the camera so your face can be seen on replay. Imagine that you, the other actor, and the camera are positioned in a triangle. When you are showing a product, for example, hold it up in the general direction of the camera rather than turning to the other actor and thrusting it in her face.

★ Sometimes at commercial auditions they will bring three people into the audition room at once. In particular, they like to do this for what I call "personality" spots that do not involve anything more than you being a happy camper. If they have three people come in at once, and if you have any leeway, try to position yourself in the middle. That way the other two actors will have to orient themselves to you.

★ If you are being videotaped in an audition, you will be asked prior to the first take to "state your name." What that means is that you should look into the lens of the camera as if it is a friend and say who you are. Think of it as a warm handshake, an introduction rather than mere cold information.

★ If you're handling a product, such as a bottle of aspirin or a container of juice, don't gesture with it as you are speaking. The viewer will focus on your hand bobbing around and will be distracted.

VIDEOTAPING

Videotape is used in auditions for commercials virtually 100 percent of the time and, to a lesser degree, in casting movies and TV shows. If you are living in, say, Philadelphia and a Hollywood movie is coming to shoot in your city, the producers may want to cast local actors for smaller roles. It is customary for a local casting director to call in local actors, put them on videotape for later consideration by the director. You can figure that, in the earliest auditions for a movie or TV project, you are more likely to be videotaped than in later (callback) auditions. In commercials, the auditions are videotaped straight through the entire process.

BODY LANGUAGE

★ In humans, the sense of sight is more powerful than the sense of hearing. What we see is going to create a strong and possibly overriding first impression. This is why body language is so important to actors. Your body gives voice to your inner true self. If you are worried or afraid, your body will express that. A nervous self-doubting actor will either not gesture enough or will tend to over-gesticulate. He will appear to be slightly out of sync with his body and he will either not smile enough or his smile will tend to be "tight" or forced. Some actors, like Woody Allen and Charlie Chaplin for instance, have found fame by purposely emphasizing this kind of physical anxiety, but for most of us it is a liability, not an asset.

★ Your body language is a powerful tool, particularly in the audition room where anxiety is likely to hang like frost on the windows. Nobody enjoys the audition process, including the auditors. If a nervous actor walks into the audition room, it creates additional tension. Walk into the room and put them at ease and you are already halfway along the path to getting cast. The idea is for you to make the casting director, director, producer, and writers glad that you showed up today. You want to communicate to them, "It's okay now. I'm here and will take care of playing this role for you."

★ The first step toward gaining control over body language is to understand that it is an expression of something. You need to focus on the chicken, not the egg. You cannot relax by ordering yourself to relax. You cannot make yourself gesture easily by ordering yourself to do so. A person who is comfortable with himself will tend to project a reassuring body language.

THE SMILE

Have you ever considered what the human smile is all about in evolutionary terms? If you were a Martian visiting Earth what would you make of the human smile? Why is it that you and I tend to be more comfortable with people who smile than people who do not? Why do mothers smile at their babies so much? Why is it that a baby's smile is universally trustworthy, but the smile of an aggressive salesman is not?

A warm and truthful smile says to the other person, "Trust me. I like you, and you like me. I won't hurt you." But a forced smile can send a mixed message. It can say simultaneously, "I won't hurt you" and "Don't trust this smile." Often, politicians will put on what I call a "professional smile." Former president Richard Nixon's smile, for instance, was generally forced. He seemed uncomfortable with himself and ill at ease and his smile and body language reflected that. A smile is a reflection of mood.

★ If you are feeling good about yourself and are excited by the audition process, you will be more likely to smile with warmth and authenticity.

THE CASTING COUCH

★ The Hollywood casting couch is something of a myth. The vast majority of casting directors are professionals who would not dream of putting the moves on an auditioning actor. Still, there is the very rare exception. Just use common sense, okay? If a casting director (or agent or director or producer) specifically asks you to kiss him in an audition or to disrobe or to do anything other than act, run screaming from the room.

HANDLING A REQUEST FOR NUDITY

★ I recommend that you have it clear in your own mind whether or not you would ever consider nudity. That way you will be prepared when the issue comes up, as it probably will at some point. Let's say you are generally opposed but might consider it if you were cast in an important role in a big studio movie. In that event, the movie is no doubt going to be approved by Screen Actors Guild, and SAG has firm rules about actors and nudity, beginning with the audition. Even if you are not yet a member of SAG, you can expect to be treated with the same respect that a union member would. For starters, SAG actresses do not disrobe at auditions unless there are other women there. It is all approved in advance by agents and casting directors and is handled with sensitivity. Before you begin actual shooting on the movie, all details having to do with nudity are spelled out in your contract. The point is that you should never be surprised by a request for nudity. You should know in advance that it is expected, and you should have control over the way it is handled.

★ Now let's say you are a new actor and a director for a non-union student film asks you to do nudity. You have no union protection and you're on your own. I would advise that you not disrobe unless there is another woman present. Take a girlfriend with you to the audition if you intend to disrobe. If you are cast, make it clear in advance to the director what your parameters are regarding nudity. Most actresses I know who have had trouble with nudity got into their situation because they had not spelled out in advance what was going to happen.

★ Low-budget and no-budget films are the main problem as far as nudity goes. Auditions may be in someone's apartment for example. I knew of one situation where the auditions were literally in a male director's bedroom. I knew of one film in which actresses were videotaped nude in audition because the movie dealt with strippers. The movie never got made, but I presume the director still has that videotape. That kind of thing would make me nervous.

★ If you ever feel intimidated at an audition or on a set, threaten to walk away, and be prepared to mean it. One of my former students told me that a director casually asked her to disrobe at an audition and, when she balked, he sighed and rolled his eyes and said, "I thought you were a professional." Don't fall for that kind of line. Professionals are definitely not expected to disrobe casually. Another student told me of being on location in a low-budget film in Northern California. It was at night near the ocean. The director got a new and fresh idea about how a scene should be played in the moonlight and, on the moment, asked her to play the scene nude. She did it and was overcome with remorse, which is why I came to find out about it. The thing is that she allowed herself to be intimidated by the insinuation that if she was a pro, it was no big deal to get naked. That is simply not so.

VOICE PROJECTION

★ Breathing may come naturally to a baby, but adults sometimes have to learn how to breathe all over again. For actors, of course, breathing correctly is essential. A painter would not want to paint with a hard and dried-out brush, and you do not want to act with a tight, misplaced voice. If you are breathing correctly, you will tend to be more relaxed and you will find that projection of your voice is ever so much easier. There is an old saying that says, "An arrow will hit the target unless you do something to get in its way."

★ If you want to learn how to project properly, simply lie on the floor on your back and relax. It's impossible to breathe incorrectly from that position. Now, while you are on the floor, call out toward the ceiling, "Ho!" Again, "Ho!" Notice that the power is in your diaphragm? Put your hand on your diaphragm so you can feel it, and then try the exercise again. That is how correct voice projection feels.

★ "I can't hear you!"

★ My first singing teacher used to tell me that nobody has to teach a bird how to sing. It is naturally designed by nature to make lovely sounds. So, too, are humans. What you need to do is get out of the way and allow the sound to come out. This is true for general speech as well as singing. Relaxation is the key.

★ How old are you? Twenty-eight? Did you know you still sound like a ten-year-old girl? You have this little tiny voice and are not breathing deeply. I think this is more than a technical matter of projection. To me, an adult who sounds like a child is saying to the world, "Don't take me seriously."

ACCENTS

★ In audition situations, don't use an extreme accent unless you are specifically asked to do so. Just because there is a reference in the dialogue to your character being originally from Georgia, that doesn't mean you have to automatically layer on a thick southern accent. I don't have an accent and I was born and raised in Georgia. Too often actors in audition want to use an accent to suggest characterization, but it backfires on them. When auditors hear an accent, they tend to focus on it and you run the risk of being viewed as a caricature.

LAUGHTER

★ Laughter is largely a factor of mood. It is an awful experience for an auditor to watch a nervous actor try to muster up a big belly laugh. She's nervous and therefore she feels humorless and grim. Her laugh sounds forced and hard. My advice is that, unless you can laugh with genuine emotion or you are specifically asked to laugh in the audition, don't try to make a vocal laugh at all.

KISSING

★ If you have to do a kissing scene in an audition, don't get overly physical. For one thing, you'll have a script in your hand. If you try to read a script and also kiss somebody, you'll get all tangled up. It is okay to "indicate" a kiss in audition and in early rehearsals. Use an air kiss or maybe just a peck. Or perhaps instead of a kiss, gently touch your scene partner's cheek.

Rehearsal

Rehearsal is where the actors and the director work on things without an audience watching. It is where you try things that may not ultimately be part of your performance. It is usually an alternately thrilling, terrifying, fascinating and boring experience. It can last for weeks or even months in the case of Broadway shows. For nonpaying plays, rehearsal typically takes place at night, on the presumption that the actors have day jobs. Under Equity contract, rehearsals happen in the daytime because actors are being paid for full-time employment.

There are many different approaches to rehearsal. Some actors and directors like to work improvisationally, slowly adjusting to the written text, and some like to stick like glue to the text from the start. Some actors arrive at the first rehearsal with their entire role already memorized; some actors wait until final rehearsals to learn their lines and get completely off book.

New actors tend to be very influenced by their acting teachers when it comes to rehearsal techniques but, gradually, they develop their own personal, even eccentric, ways of working. For some actors, it makes a big difference whether their lines in the script are underlined in red or highlighted in yellow. For example, I'm one who does not like or enjoy a lot of improvisation in rehearsal, although I've done my share of it in the past. Nor do I particularly enjoy rehearsal that goes on for months on end. I like two or three weeks of no-nonsense rehearsal max. Yet I have actor friends who would happily stay in rehearsal for years, trying this and that. If they had their way, the play would never open.

I prefer to start right out on the first day of rehearsal by taking the words the playwright wrote and work on the challenge of justifying them. But I know people who prefer to view the playwright's words as a suggestion rather than a mandate for as long as possible. I like for the director to give me a lot of latitude in rehearsal, but I have friends who don't like to do anything without directorial input and approval. I remember a director in New York who, during rehearsal, wanted me to bring in "five things your character would have in his pants pocket." Yuck! I hate that kind of stuff. But some people eat it up, and that's okay, too.

REHEARSING FOR DIFFERENT MEDIUMS

Movies don't have much, if any, rehearsal. For day players—actors with one or two scenes and few lines, rehearsal is a rarity. You are expected to know your lines and be ready to go when you show up on the set. Some movie stars are powerful enough to demand at least one read-through with the entire cast on some day prior to the start of filming, but even that isn't something you should count on.

Television situation comedies rehearse for a week as the writers rewrite, and then the show is taped in front of a live audience a couple of times. They take the best takes from each show and put them together in the final edit.

A soap opera is, in my opinion, the most grueling kind of show for actors because a full-hour show is taped each day. Compare this to the relatively leisurely production schedule for a movie, which can range from a month to a year or more to come up with an hour and a half of finished film. The production schedule for nighttime one-hour episodic television shows is typically a week. On a soap, the actors arrive extremely early in the morning and start with a read-through of the script that was given to them the night before. There are several runs of the script, with the writers rewriting all the time. There is a lot of pressure to get your energy up to performance level quickly. After lunch, taping starts for real. I had a role for a while on the soap opera *Days of Our Lives,* and it was perfectly normal for the producers to give me fifteen pages of dialogue on Monday for taping on Tuesday. Then on Tuesday, they would rewrite half of it. By the time taping began, I would be almost dizzy from the changes.

Television commercials usually don't have rehearsal at all. Most of them are ten to thirty seconds long and are shot in a single day. You show up on the set and perform the same short bit over and over and over again. It is not unusual for an actor in a commercial to do upward of twenty or thirty takes. Also, next time you watch TV, note how many quick cuts there are in the typical commercial. Every time you see one of those, it means there was a new setup at the shoot. They had to move the camera, reset the lights and so on. That is why, on a cost-per-filmed-second basis, TV commercials actually cost more to produce than most movies.

True story about rehearsal: I did my first professional acting at the Penn State Theater Festival in 1970, where I played the role of Tony, the young leading man, in Kaufman and Hart's play *You Can't Take it With You.* I was fresh out of acting school (the American Academy of Dramatic Arts in New York) and was somewhat idealistic. I was taught that the actor should honor the playwright and bring his words to life. I had all these scenes with Alice, the character in the play who was in love with me. We had a lot of cooing and kissing in the moonlight to do. Well, I didn't factor in the possibility that the actress playing Alice would balk.

We got into rehearsal, and I quickly discovered that she didn't much care for me on a personal or professional level, was far more experienced an actor than I was, and that she didn't want to be playing the role she was playing. Instead of dealing with me in a loving way as the playwrights instructed, she kept her distance and was physically tense. She told me precisely how I was to kiss her, instructing me how my lips should go and all that. I was intimidated as an actor and as a man. I turned to the director, and he was no help at all. Rehearsal was for me a miserable experience, and then we opened the play to sold-out houses. She still hated me. Everything that was happening in rehearsal flew in the face of what I had been taught. Where was the idealism? Where was the dedication to the playwright? Though in my later career, I would encounter independent-minded actors many more times, I was never taught how to deal with someone who did not want to do what was written in the script.

Halfway through the run of the play, I finally learned one of the most important acting lessons: Play off the reality of what your scene partner is doing. Maybe I had heard that at the Academy, but it didn't register at the time and, anyway, I don't think they had my situation in mind. At any rate, I remember the night and the moment I learned this one. It was time for one of those kisses. I took a step toward Alice, and she was supposed to come eagerly into my embrace. Instead, she took a small, almost unnoticeable step backward. On previous nights, I had pursued her because it was time for the kiss. On that particular night, something inside me snapped. She stepped back, and, instead of pursuing her, I dropped my hands to my sides, took a step backward myself, and smiled at her. I knew we had to kiss, and I was simply not going to chase this lady around the stage one moment more. She got the message when the audience began to chuckle. I could see a slight panic in her eyes. I stood there and smiled broader, waiting for her. The audience chuckle turned into a laugh. She came into my arms, and I kissed her. My way. I did with my lips whatever I thought was right.

I never had another moment of trouble with her. From that performance on, she behaved herself and acted like a woman in love. She still hated me, I'm sure, but she learned to respect me as an actor.

Could the problem have been fixed in rehearsal? Probably. As I say, I have since acted many times with actors who were not doing what the playwright suggested. Now I know what to do about it.

The field notes that follow are a reflection of what I know to be the real-world issues involved in rehearsal. If I had had the benefit of such notes back in 1970 at Penn State, I am quite certain I would have been more ready for opening night.

FIELD NOTES

APPROACHING THE SCRIPT

★ Don't commit too quickly to a performance. When you first read through the scene with your partner, remain mentally agile. Listen to what your partner is saying; pay attention to nuance; experiment with readings that may run counter to the obvious. You have to build a characterization like you build a house. Don't start painting the trim until you have a firm foundation in place.

★ When you are rehearsing Shakespeare, it is useful to paraphrase the language into contemporary speech early on. You'll be surprised at the insights you gain from this exercise.

★ Don't worry about iambic pentameter yet. Just try to figure out what you're saying. What's the point of your lines? We'll get to the meter later. Speak simply and clearly and with purpose.

★ Try running through the scene speaking gibberish instead of the lines. It will be fun and will help you uncover gaps in intention. Remember, you should play an action until something happens to make you play a different action. When you speak gibberish, it makes it more difficult to "fake it" with actions and intentions. You are reducing your acting to pure action with this exercise. What you should discover as you play with gibberish is that you will occasionally lose track of where you are in the scene. Most often, the place where you lose track is where you are losing connection with your actions and intentions.

★ Here's a good exercise. Take that intense and depressing mono-logue and try doing it as a comic stand-up routine. Then go back to doing it straight. You'll be surprised at the new insights you will get.

★ Your character is a little salty maybe, but she does not routinely cuss like a sailor. Yet moments after entering this comedic scene, the playwright has her exclaim "Shit! Fuck! Piss!" That's extreme language, wouldn't you agree? Well you are not presently justi-fying it. You are saying the words all right, but without enough passion to support that degree of profanity. I have a hunch that you are personally uncomfortable cussing like that. As a rehear-sal technique, try isolating just the words "Shit! Fuck! Piss!" Walk around the stage and say them over and over until it feels like you have connected with the profanity in a personal way. Then start the scene again at the top.

★ You are in the earliest stage of rehearsal, still holding the script. The trick at this point is to find emotional through-lines. Emotion tends to lead to action. In order to build your scene and characterization, it is wise to pay close attention to your emotional responses to your partner right from the start. Do you notice that, when your partner is giving you a line, you tend to drop away emotionally and follow along in the script? Get your head up and listen to him. Get the feeling he is sending in your direction, and then glance down to see which of your words come next.

★ When you refer aloud to your character, use the first person. From the first time you pick up the script, speak of the charac-ter as "I," not "he" or "she." As long as you refer to him in the third person, you are keeping an intellectual distance between yourself and your character. Remember, what you are pursuing are the emotions that underlie the character. It is essential that you break down any intellectual distance you may have from the character.

★ When first researching a role ask yourself these two questions: "How am I like the character? How am I different from the character?" At this point in rehearsal, you will still have an intellectual distance from the character, which is okay. This is really the first step toward changing the third-person reference into a first-person reference. By the time you get up on your feet with script in hand, your references to the character should be 100 percent in the first person.

STICKING TO THE SCRIPT

★ The dialogue in the script is not merely a suggestion, love. Those are the words you have to say. Nothing more and nothing less. You can change them in early-rehearsal improvisation, but at some point, you have to come back to what the playwright wrote.

STAGE DIRECTIONS

★ When you read a play, it's almost always okay to ignore the stage directions that are printed in italics. Ninety-nine percent of the time those notes are descriptions of what was done in previous productions. That doesn't mean you have to do it in your production. I read somewhere that actor Christopher Walken not only crosses out all the words in italics when he begins rehearsal, he also eliminates all the punctuation!

ENTER LAUGHING

Carl Reiner wrote one of my favorite comedies, *Enter Laughing*. It is about this New York kid who longs to become an actor and gets involved with this low-rent acting company. At his audition for the company's director, he takes script in hand and starts acting out the stage directions in his best Laurence Olivier voice. First thing he says is, "Enter laughing"! Cracks me up every time I read it. He hasn't learned yet that actors should just ignore those stage directions.

MEMORIZING LINES

★ Here's a trick for quickly memorizing your lines I learned thirty years ago from an interview I read with the great actor Ralph Richardson. Sit at a table with a yellow lined pad and a felt-tip pen. Lay your script open on the table next to the pad. Using a large index card, cover up the dialogue in the script. Now, slowly move the card down, exposing the lines of the other character. Write your responding line on the pad—two lines high. Move the card down the page, exposing your line. Look to see if you wrote it correctly. If not, write the entire line again. No fair correcting individual words. If you get it wrong, rewrite it. Then move the card down again, exposing the next line, and so on. I'm not positive why this technique works, but I think it has something to do with the part of your brain you use to instruct your hand to write. It is a different part than the one you use to simply memorize. Writing the lines two lines high for some reason makes a bigger impression on your brain. Maybe because we do not typically write two lines high and so it is mentally a little jarring. All I know is that I have used this device to learn entire lead roles almost overnight. It is a wonderful trick.

WORKING ON ACCENTS

★ In an actual production, an accent may be very important, and so it is a good idea to start playing with it early in rehearsal. If you are lucky, your production will employ a dialogue coach who is an expert at whatever accent you need to master. If you are on your own and must come up with, say, a Cockney accent, try first to find a British person who can help you. Next, purchase one of the many available accent tapes on the market. You can find them on-line if you surf around, or you can contact one of the major theatrical bookstores such as the Drama Book Shop in New York City. Finally, you can rent movies and study accents. If I were trying to come up with Cockney, for instance, I would check out some of Michael Caine's early work. My personal opinion is that the least productive thing you can do to develop an accent is to start asking other actors in the production how to do it. If you go that route, you run the risk that your fellow actors will start suggesting how you should perform the role.

★ The southern accent is an attitude that expresses itself in a certain rhythm. It is a way of coming at life, more than a layered-on cadence or phrasing emphasis.

★ This character is very Mississippi. You've got way too much Vermont in there.

LINE READINGS

★ Experienced directors know that it is considered bad form and is a kind of insult to tell an actor precisely how to say a particular line. In the biz, this is known as giving a "line reading." If you find yourself working with a director who is giving line readings, it is okay to take her aside and explain that you would prefer she not do that. Don't correct her in front of the other actors, of course. Speaking from my personal experience, I have most often encountered the line reading problem on commercial sets. The client will want a particular emphasis on a particular word for sales-impact reasons. In that case, I listen politely and try to comply. They mean well and I'm getting paid a lot. I'll say it like they want it if they insist, just as long as the checks cash.

GETTING ALONG WITH THE OTHER ACTORS

★ Never direct the other actor in rehearsal.

REHEARSAL DRESS

★ You're getting ready for a date in this scene, aren't you? Well, you're going to feel more like something special is happening if you put on a dress instead of those floppy jeans. Show off your legs a bit, try to impress the man. You don't have to fully costume yourself for rehearsal, but it is a good idea to dress up enough to help you find the feelings of the character. A skirt instead of jeans, heels instead of sneakers, or a shirt/tie instead of a T-shirt. If your character wears a unique hat or an ascot or vest, try wearing that during rehearsal.

★ Do you own a girdle by chance, Lori? When you are rehearsing one of these Elizabethan characters, remember that in that era women were physically constricted by their corsets and such. If you wear a girdle or even one of those therapeutic back braces in rehearsal, it will force you to stiffen your back and to stand more erect. It will cause you to feel different and that should help your character development.

★ DRESS THE PART

My costume for the play was a tuxedo, and because I liked the way it made me feel and thought it made me look dashing, I wore it during rehearsals. Then one day late in rehearsal a very experienced actor in the cast named David Spielberg took me aside and suggested that maybe my tux should not be so neat and pretty and freshly pressed. He pointed out to me that at this particular moment in the play my character is worried that his engagement is being called off. He said that, prior to my entrance, Tony might well have been out walking the street for hours on end and that maybe he would have loosened his tie or something. He pointed out that it might work better as a character element if I was wearing a disheveled tux instead of a freshly pressed one. I knew instantly that he was correct. David, if you are reading these words, I thank you again—thirty years after the fact—for the excellent acting advice.

PROPS

★ I appreciate that your character might habitually chew on a toothpick, and I applaud you for thinking of it. But you look like you are personally uncomfortable with the choice. If you're going to use the toothpick that way, then I suggest you put one in your mouth off and on during the day. Make it second nature to shift the thing back and forth in your teeth. Remember, even with it in your mouth you are going to have to speak clearly.

ADRENALINE

★ There was an actress I worked with in summer stock who was a nervous wreck. She had excess adrenaline running through her during performance. In one show there was a gag in which she had to slap my sunburned back. The lady damn near killed me! She had no sense of her own strength during performance. Keep in mind that performance creates extra adrenaline. Be careful with physicality on stage.

★ Be careful with that broken cup! If you fling that thing around on stage the way you are doing, someone may get injured. An actress in one of my Los Angeles classes once got cut in the middle of a scene when her partner threw a ceramic dish at her. It hit her in the calf and she ultimately required stitches for the wound. Be very careful when handling props that can do real physical damage. You have so much adrenaline flowing on stage that it is easy to get hurt.

REHEARSING FIGHT SCENES

★ Please be very careful when rehearsing fight scenes. When you act, you have a lot of adrenaline flowing, and it will get even worse when you are in front of an actual audience. Remember that the person who is on the receiving end of the violence is the one who controls the flow of action. If you have to throw another actor across the stage, you don't really throw him at all. He controls his own throw. The same principle applies to a stage slap. I have seen actors damn near kill one another with stage slaps. You have to work slaps out carefully. The audience's eyes will go to the person being slapped. If he or she recoils, the audience will accept that the character was hit. It really is a matter of choreography.

★ David, is that a real gun? I do not believe you brought a real gun into a scene! I don't care if it's not loaded. Never ever bring a real and functional gun on stage unless the firing pin has been totally filed down and the thing won't fire no matter what. You scared the bejeezus out of me!

★ If your scene involves the threat of violence with a knife, use either a rubber knife or something that is very blunt. Also choreograph the fight extremely carefully.

PLAYWRIGHTS

★ If you are cast in a Harold Pinter play, you will come at it in a different way than you would if you were cast in a play by Sam Shepard or Tennessee Williams or Shakespeare. You don't act a style per se, but there is a difference in feel and approach between most of the major writers. Sam Shepard's characters are invariably and symbolically wrapped in the American flag for instance. Shepard's plays are acted with no pastels. It is all bright and vibrant colors. Shepard's characters are mythic, Old West good guys and bad guys, very bold. And his women are red-blooded and lusty. Tennessee Williams's plays are full of metaphors and poetry. His characters are far more introspective than most. With Pinter, you have to figure out what to do about those famous silences.

> The famous Japanese animation director Hayao Miyazaki talks about the value of "ma." Ma is the space in between the sound of the claps when you clap your hands. That space is not simply nothing. It is something. You can fill "ma" with emotion and intention. Harold Pinter's plays rely a lot on "ma."

★ I recall an interview with actor Joe Mantegna in which he talked about the challenges of acting in David Mamet's plays. He said that invariably during the rehearsal process, he would become convinced that Mamet had finally dropped the ball with this line or that. He would be unable to justify it and would want Mamet to change the line. But just as invariably, if he would just trust the line and keep saying it, he would discover that Mamet was right all along. The lesson here is that you need to know your writer. In my early acting career, I performed in many original plays off and off-off Broadway. Some of them were just god awful, but I learned so much from them that I cherish the experience. It is one thing to act in a play by, say, Eugene O'Neill and quite another to act in a new play by an untried playwright. With O'Neill, you know going in that the play works, and you only have to find the key. With a new writer, you cannot presume that.

> A Tennessee Williams play is like poetry. He wrote language that almost floats.

★ Playwrights August Strindberg, Harold Pinter, David Mamet, and Sam Shepard all have something in common. Their work contains an undertow of potential violence. When Robert Woodruff directed the first production of Shepard's *True West* in San Francisco, he used the image of a prizefight as inspiration when staging the scenes between the brothers. Watching one of Shepard's plays is not an altogether comfortable feeling. You have the strong impression that somebody is going to grab somebody else by the throat pretty soon.

WHEN THE PLAYWRIGHT IS PRESENT

★ When you work on original material, the playwright will frequently be present at rehearsals. The usual chain of command is that the playwright talks to the director and the director talks to the actors. You, as an actor, do not want to put the playwright in the position of actually directing or telling you how to play a scene.

DIRECTING

★ Next time you are looking for a scene assignment in acting class, why don't you try directing instead of acting? You will learn a lot about acting if you have to help other actors build a scene effectively. It is sort of like the difference between being a football coach standing on the sidelines and a quarterback on the field of play. You are both calling plays, but the coach doesn't have to worry about somebody sacking him. When you direct a scene instead of acting in it, you have an objective distance and a new perspective.

★ Some of the best directors—and writers for that matter—were actors first. As an actor you learn to orient strictly to impulse and emotion. As a director or writer, you still have to do that but you need to structure things more conceptually. Stanislavsky himself was first an actor, as was Shakespeare.

GETTING IN TOUCH WITH YOUR INNER ANIMAL

★ Humans are animals, too, don't forget. Just like tigers and elk and wolves, we are competitive and hungry. Don't deny the animal within. Tapping into it can sometimes lead to a very compelling characterization. Remember Brando in *A Streetcar Named Desire?*

★ Life for your character is a contact sport. She never ever relaxes. Try approaching your characterization more physically. Get out of your head and join the other wild animals in the woods.

USING THE OTHER CHARACTERS' LINES

★ Look to the other characters' lines for ideas about how to play your role. The best clues about your character often come out of the mouths of other characters. She just said, "You can't control everything, Mary, even though you wish you could." What does that bring to mind? For me, I think of Martha Stewart.

PLAYING CRAZY

★ Crazy people don't think they're crazy, Leslie. Your character sincerely believes that she can bring Elvis Presley back to life. You can't play her as if she has a screw loose. The best approach to playing this character is to make concrete plans for your first face-to-face meeting with the King.

★ Blanche is on the precipice of insanity, afraid that she will be discovered to be crazy before she succeeds in getting Stella to leave Stanley. You are still too lucid. Work harder to cover the craziness. Try to come off as normal. It is sort of like, if you want to cry, try not to cry. Or, if you want to act drunk, try to act sober. If you want to act crazy, try to act sane.

PLAYING A RACIST

★ Your character is a racist. I was born and raised in the segregated South and have seen racism up close. The way to play it is to dismiss the black person as a nonperson. It is too simplistic and too much of a false stereotype to snarl and bare your teeth and, anyway, most racists don't act like that. Members of wild-eyed white supremacist groups might snarl and rage so as to impress one another, but your garden-variety racist basically just tries not to engage very deeply with anybody of another ethnicity. Most racists I have known are actually quite gentle.

PLAYING A SUICIDAL CHARACTER

★ *Night Mother* is a one-act real-time play at the end of which the central character commits suicide. You can't wait until the moment of the suicide in order to motivate it. She knows at the top of the play she is going to kill herself. Suicide is most often premeditated. It is not something done impulsively. People who commit suicide usually plan it and talk about it for a long time. They might write long good-bye letters about it, even books. They plan it just like planning a long vacation.

PLAYING A CHILD-LIKE CHARACTER

★ Larry, your character is a child-like man. The trick to playing him is to remember that you can't multi-task. Lenny has a one-track mind and he is an innocent. Every time he asks George to tell him about the rabbits, it is like he has never heard about the rabbits before. Lenny is like a kid who wants to hear the same bedtime story a hundred times. Every time he hears it, he laughs in the same places and gets scared in the same places.

THIRD-PERSON PERSPECTIVE

★ Richard, I believe you have gotten into trouble here by trying to portray rather than reveal the character. You have placed the character in a third-person perspective in your head. It looks like you have an idea how you want him to move and talk and you are trying to make it come out that way. Well you can't. If you are thinking about how you should move and talk, then you're not thinking about what you are trying to achieve in the piece. Who are you talking to? Why are you telling him this? During the speech, on a moment to moment basis, are you making any progress with him? You haven't justified the character in terms of yourself, the character's intention, or the present moment.

TIME PERIOD

★ This play takes place in the 1950s, an era that was not nearly as sexually liberated as today. Back then, homosexuality was still considered a disease, a perversion. Today, most people don't think like that. This woman you're playing is living in a less-enlightened time and would blush and react with astonishment if she found out a friend was a lesbian.

RELIGION

★ Joyce, I noticed that your character mentions Ash Wednesday in the scene. That says to me she is Catholic. And if you agree that she's Catholic, you will help yourself as an actor if you make her a good and devout Catholic. That way your attraction to Polo is not only a no-no because he is your husband's brother. Screwing around with him may also land you in hell. It is always best to make acting choices that cause you the most problems.

SMOKING

★ If you don't smoke but your character does, talk to the director about coming up with a replacement habit for the character. Some of the most produced plays out there were written back before people believed all those rumors about smoking and lung cancer. Times have changed since then. You should not have to endanger your own health in order to portray a character with a bad habit.

EXPOSING THE CHARACTER

★ Your work ethic is showing, Lindsay. I can tell that you are one of those people who is, by God, going to get it right if it is the last thing you ever do! Unfortunately, acting doesn't work like that. You can't wrestle the role to the ground. You can't overpower it. Acting is a process of exposing, of allowing. It is not a process of causing.

★ Acting is an interpretative art. An actor is not merely a blank piece of paper that a playwright writes on.

★ Nonactors mistakenly believe that acting is a process of hiding. By that reasoning, you "become the character," stepping outside of your own self. This is impossible. You can't be anybody but yourself, and you must be yourself one hundred percent of the time, day and night, awake and asleep, all your life long. You do not hide behind a character; you expose the character through yourself. You find in yourself those aspects of the character that you find important, and you tell the truth about them. It requires a lot of courage to be a good actor. Acting is a process of *allowing,* not *causing.*

PSYCHOLOGICAL VISIBILITY

Every actor knows that when you act on stage you must speak loudly enough to be heard and orient yourself physically so that the audience can get a good look at you, right? Well, there is another, arguably even more important, aspect to being seen, one that is much trickier and can make the difference between a performance that is merely adequate and one that has real power: Psychological visibility.

To make yourself psychologically visible is to display your authentic self to the world. You wear who you are on your sleeve and you run the risk that some people will like it and some will not. Each of us is defined by our values and, by extension, our emotions; these things dictate how we interact with the world around us and are a component of our self-image. A person who is psychologically visible is one who is in touch with herself.

Why is this idea important to acting? Because when we act, we say to the audience, in effect, "I understand this about this character." When the audience laughs, cries, and applauds, it is saying, "I see what you mean." It is not enough to simply deliver an accurate characterization. A character does not exist in limbo. It is tied to the heart and soul of the actor who creates it. The power in acting has as much to do with the essence of the actor who is playing the part as it does with the character being portrayed. This is why acting requires courage.

BEING YOURSELF

★ A psychological subjectivist is a person whose self-esteem is dependent upon the opinions of others. If you approach your career like that, you'll run around trying to be what you think everybody wants to see. It is better to wear who you are on your sleeve. Be 100 percent of who you are. Some people will like it and some will not. But they won't forget you. Consider major stars like Hoffman, Streep, De Niro, Judi Dench, Anthony Hopkins. Each of them has almost a tactile sense of themselves.

IMPOSING YOURSELF ON YOUR CHARACTER

★ You're on your way to becoming a personality actor rather than a character actor. I'm noticing that every character you play tends to be like you in real life. They walk the same and sound the same. All that is changing are the words. Television is chock full of personality actors, many of whom come from a background of stand-up comedy. I'm presuming you want to be the kind of actor who plays a wide range of roles, from Shakespeare to contemporary comedy. If you do, you need to listen more to the rhythms of your characters and pay more attention to their values. You can't impose yourself on them so much. Yes, you want to find the character in yourself and yourself in the character and then tell the truth about that. But you do not want to make all of your characters behave like you do in your real life.

★ I'm going to give you a criticism that sounds like a compliment: You are a sweetheart. You are kind and loving and try to get along with people all the time. The problem is that your character is a bullshit artist. You can't have it both ways. It is not a reflection on your innate goodness to allow yourself to be a bullshit artist when you are playing this character.

★ You are approaching rehearsal more like a director than an actor, Alan. I can feel you dictating to your character rather than listening to him. You want to be very cautious about imposing yourself too much on the character. Listen to him and he'll tell you what to do.

★ An actor in one of my Los Angeles classes was methodically eliminating all blasphemy from every scene he presented. When I asked him about it, he explained that he was born-again and had a deal with God, which apparently included that the actor not voice any blasphemy. I told him that it is very nice about him finding God and all, but the character he's playing does not have such a deal going on. It is an acting error to impose your own personal value system on your character.

GOOD VERSUS EVIL

Our current political leaders have a tendency to divide the world into people that are good and evil, those that are for us or against us. Actors need to be very cautious about doing that sort of thing. For actors, people are just people and each, in his own way, is trying to make it through life. It is an actor's job to understand what is underneath all human behavior, even if that behavior is considered evil by ninety percent of the people in the world. On September 11, 2001, for example, terrorists crashed jets into New York's World Trade Center. They were immediately labeled evil by U.S. leaders. If I were cast as one of those terrorists, I would try to understand why it was a higher value for me to commit suicide that way than to live another day to fight the good fight. We as a human tribe learn nothing if our shamans categorize some people as good and some as evil. Actors are more like religious leaders in this regard. It is all the family of man, for better or worse. It is our job to understand and then to tell the tribe what we know.

★ Never comment on your character. The character you are playing may not be somebody you would want to spend time with in real life. She may be constantly ill-tempered and caustic, for example. But remember, she is doing the best she thinks she can for herself. Her toxic behavior could be, for her, a defensive shield. My point is that as an actor you should find the justification for the behavior without standing in judgement of it. If you think your character is a despicable human being, you still need to find her survival mechanism. Play even an unlikeable character with love and respect.

★ A villain is the hero of his own life.

★ Your character is a victim of sexual abuse, and you are handling it in entirely too healthy a way for the scene. If you were a victim of sex abuse in real life, you'd go to a psychiatrist and hopefully work things out. In the first place, your character can't afford therapy. She has allowed the abuse to fester inside her and develop to the point where it is blocking any possibilities of intimacy in her life. She's full of self-hatred because of the abuse. She's pissed off and thinks she is worthless. She's blaming herself for being abused. Do not impose your own survival strategies on your character. Rather, try to justify and motivate your character's behavior. She has done the best she can in life after all.

★ You are a person who is uncomfortable expressing anger. This is a matter for you to work out with your psychotherapist. Your character here is a hothead and a loose cannon. That is precisely why he landed on death row, and that is why I assigned this scene to you. I knew going in that you would have trouble with this role, and I wanted you to confront it. What you have done is convert hotheaded anger into dry anger, and that's not okay. You have turned your character into the kind of person that would likely not have wound up on death row.

★ Your personal life is intruding into your work. You may personally be having trouble with men, but that is not true of this character you are playing. She is deeply and comfortably and passionately in love. You're going to have to release all that personal anger you're carrying around before the curtain goes up.

★ You know what's wrong with your characterization? You're trying to make your character too likeable. She's spoiled, a princess. She's irritating in her self-absorption. Go ahead and tap into that aspect of your own personality.

★ Jennifer, you are a very rational and together person. But the character you are playing is a mess. Please stop trying to make her rational like you. In her irrationality you will discover immense charm.

★ Maggie wears a slip in this scene. That's just the way it is. If you don't think you look good in a slip, then get over it. We don't care about how you think you look in a slip anyway. We're interested in how *Maggie* feels about it.

RESPECTING YOUR CHARACTER

★ Never condescend to your character. If you are playing a character who is, for example, not the sharpest tack in the box, you would not want to play him as stupid. A stupid person doesn't think he is stupid. The general rule is that you should give every character the same respect you give yourself when it comes to doing your best in life.

★ What do you want us to understand about this character, Rachelle? Why should we care about her? Honestly, right now I don't think I would care one way or the other if she came into my life. Every life is exciting.

SEXUAL ORIENTATION

★ New actors sometimes become uncomfortable if they are called upon to play a character with a different sexual orientation from their own. It is not difficult to play a gay character if you are, in life, straight, or vice versa. Love is love. Wanting to be held means the same thing regardless of orientation. The song from the movie *Casablanca* had it right: "A kiss is still a kiss..." Yes, there are flamboyant or theatrical characters of both orientations, but you should not back away from that either. As long as you approach characterization with love, even if it is an extreme or flamboyant result, you will be okay if you have true respect and love for the humanity of your character. Treat him with love and respect and so will your audience. Poke fun at him, and your audience will turn on you.

USING YOUR EXPERIENCES

★ Actors are scavengers of life experiences. If a lover leaves you, you file away the emotional experience, like a library book on a shelf. You'll be able to refer back to that emotional experience later and use it in a performance.

★ Actors are frequently embarrassing to live with because they have a tendency to study human behavior. A trip to the grocery store or a cup of coffee at a local café is, for most humans, just a regular activity. For an actor, it's a class.

★ If you hang a camera around your neck and walk down the street, you're going to see potential photographs. It will happen to you even if you aren't trying. Actors have to get like that without the camera. When you walk down the street, you have to be attuned to the nuances of human behavior around you.

★ A friend of mine went to the hairdresser and got a severely short haircut, snipping off her customary shoulder-length blonde locks. Her reasoning when I asked was that her lovely four-month-old baby kept grabbing her hair when she was nursing. From an actor's perspective, I loved the practicality of her decision. It could be a strong character element in the right play. Practicality over vanity.

★ Actors are funny humans. An actor will be in the middle of a knock-down drag-out fight with his wife or partner and, inside, he's thinking, "Hey, this is good! I can use this in a scene!"

EVOLUTIONARY PSYCHOLOGY

★ Read *The Moral Animal* by Robert Wright if you are interested in evolutionary psychology. The baseline of evolutionary psychology is that there is a clear connection between thinking, emotion, and physical action. Further, emotions are nature's executioners. We are hard-wired to respond favorably to those things that help us get into the next generation (sex for instance), but we respond unfavorably to those things that will hurt the next generation (incest for instance). All humans act to survive. That is our imperative, and our fallibility is what makes the human condition subject matter for drama. Males and females have different mating strategies. Put it all in a pot and stir over a low temperature and you have evolutionary psychology. I personally use evolutionary psychology quite a lot when I am analyzing scenes and looking for character motivation.

★ Remember the character of Gomer Pyle on TV? Remember how Jim Nabors, the actor who portrayed him, used to good-naturedly hold his head high, causing his neck and throat area to always be exposed? That kind of vulnerable interface with the world is a status transaction in which the Pyle character is low status. Consider this in evolutionary terms. Cave men and women who exposed their throats like that would have been lunch for a saber-toothed tiger. They would have died young.

PLAYING SHAKESPEARE

★ If you have never spoken Shakespeare's language aloud, try starting with the sonnets. They are short, only fourteen lines long, and they have many of the same structural issues that you'd face with longer scenes and monologues. Anyway, they're quite beautiful, and if you learn a few of them you'll probably score a lot of dates.

★ Iago, from Shakespeare's *Othello,* is a fun character to play because he's always up to something.

WOMEN IN SHAKESPEARE

You may notice that there is a dearth of good roles for midlife females in Shakespeare—women who are sexually active but mature. That's because in his day there were no actresses. Men played all the roles and had more trouble playing women in that age range. His ingenues are so richly written because young actors *could* play those roles. Roles like Kate in *The Taming of the Shrew* are pretty rare in Shakespeare.

★ I read a recent review of a New York production of Shakespeare's *Othello* in which the actor playing Iago portrayed him as longing for Desdemona but being sexually impotent. Cool choice! What it did was make Iago all the more jealous of Othello, and it justified his evil doings. I love that kind of acting choice because it is so bold.

★ Brutus was actually Caesar's son. Even Shakespeare didn't know that, but it's true, and it makes a big difference in the dynamic of the relationship between the men.

MASCULINE AND FEMININE

ANIMUS AND ANIMA

The famous psychologist Carl Jung used to talk about how each of us has within us aspects of both genders: animus (male) and anime (female).The first time I used the animus/anima idea in an acting class was with an actress who was doing a monologue from *Medea*. She was trying to explain why she had killed her own sons. This woman could not find it within herself to even relate to such a horrible thing. I talked to her about masculine and feminine and asked her to think as a man. When she did that, she could suddenly justify the killings as a matter of strategy. It was a fascinating moment for that actor's growth. We in the class saw the same actor on stage both times, saying the same words both times. But the second time she was giving up her maternal side in favor of her warrior side. Suddenly, it made sense that she would have killed her own children. I have since used this same technique with men who are too macho, women who are too lightweight, and so on. The key is understanding that there is nothing pejorative about it. We all have both sides—masculine and feminine.

★ Sarah, I can see that you are having trouble with this character and I think the reason is that she is so girlish. It looks to me like you don't want to own that potential in yourself. Women have worked very hard to be taken seriously in the world, and I can understand your resistance to hauling up the very aspects of girlishness that you may, in your real life, be working to be rid of. But the truth is that there are many women in the world like this character. They have elements of Scarlett O'Hara in them. They orient themselves to men, pretend to be weak at the appropriate times, flirt continually. For such a person, her feminine wiles are her greatest strength—not the weakness that you seem to think they are.

Playing the Scene

Playing a scene in front of an audience is to acting what cruising at 35,000 feet is to flying. In some ways it is easier than take-off, but if your engine falters, the ground is a long way down.

A scene must work on its own terms and it must work in terms of the overall story. This is true 100 percent of the time whether it is stage, film, or television, and regardless of style. This is one of the biggest challenges for an actor, in fact. You work up a scene and make it fly. It's firing on all cylinders for you and the rest of the cast, and you're pleased with yourselves. Then you discover that the final scene in Act I does not logically lead to what is necessary at the top of Act II. It's working on its own terms, but it doesn't fit into the play.

The problem can be even worse if you're shooting a movie because, in that case, you often shoot out of sequence. You film the breakup scene and then two days later film the scene where you and your lover first meet. You have to keep the logic of the story and progression of action in your head. At least with a play one scene leads to the next.

A scene will play differently each time you perform it if you are acting well. There will be variations in nuance and line interpretation from performance to performance because the actors are surprising themselves and each other. The idea is to remain loose and not to "fix" the reading of a particular line in your head. As soon as you set a line in your mind, you become more like a windup doll than an actor.

Many new actors today get themselves into trouble with the mistaken notion that if they can just be natural on stage and be truly reactive to their scene partner, that will make them a good actor. True, being natural and listening are both elements of good acting, but theatrical reality is not the same thing as regular reality. Regular reality is what you get when you visit the 7-Eleven or gas station on the corner. It may be interesting to a visiting Martian, but it has no theatrical value. People are not going to pay to watch what goes on at a convenience store. Acting is, in fact, storytelling, and there are certain elements, such as conflict, that are necessary to give a story theatrical value.

FIELD NOTES

PLAYING AN ACTION

★ In theatrical terms, playing an action means to do something in pursuit of an objective. I buy a gun because I want to rob a bank. I charm the traffic cop because I don't want him to give me a ticket. It is important that you not confuse an action with simple behavior. If I am standing in my living room scratching my head, that isn't an action unless I have lice.

> Constantin Stanislavsky defined acting as playing an action in pursuit of an objective while overcoming an obstacle.

★ Everything on stage is significant. When you stop and look out the window, it is theatrically significant. When you pause mid-sentence to re-form a thought, it is theatrically significant. Right now, you're doing those kinds of things—looking out the window and pausing mid-sentence—but there is no significance to the moment. Looking out the window is an action; what is the objective? What is the obstacle?

★ Movement on stage ideally should be organic. In other words, you will have a reason for movement. You cross the room because you want to glance out the window, or you rise from the sofa because you need to stretch your back. Maybe you move closer to your scene partner so you can speak more quietly and not wake the baby in the other room.

★ I applaud the way you are twisting and wringing your neck scarf in an effort to generate internal angst. But after a while, if you keep doing it, the scene starts to be about scarf twisting. You're getting in touch with the feeling of angst, but then you are not doing anything with the feeling. Acting is doing something in pursuit of an objective. You are making it look like this play has something to do with scarves. Your scarf twisting is only a tool in this moment. Use it and move along.

★ You must have a motivation for everything you do, including the way you cross the room! Even if you just stand there like a rock, you must motivate it. Never ever do something simply because the script says you should.

★ Stop pacing! The purpose of movement is destination. If you don't have some reason for moving from stage left to stage right, then stay put. Otherwise it will look like you are just suffering from actor nerves.

★ At the top of the scene, we discover you standing center stage, gazing straight out. What are you looking at? Right now, it seems to me like you are just standing there waiting for the other actor to say the first line. Your mind needs to be active. You need to be playing an action even before the other person says the first line.

★ Reflection and musing are not substitutes for playing an action. I can see that you are reflecting on your character's lot in life. Why? Why are you speaking of this incident at this time? What do you want? Where's the conflict? Clearly you are a sensitive man, and I applaud that, but it is not enough for the scene.

★ The playwright didn't do you any favors with this scene. It is all talk, talk, talk. The premise seems to be that these characters are so fascinating that what they say is worthy of attention. Well, I have news for you. If all you're doing is talk, talk, talk, you're going to lose twenty-five percent of your audience at intermission. Acting is doing! What are you doing? What is your objective? Where is the obstacle? What is the negotiation?

RAISING THE STAKES

★ Raise the stakes! You don't want to play boyfriend-girlfriend breakup scene number 498. You want to play *the* breakup scene of your life. The audience doesn't want to see another set of young people working out their boring lives. They want to see Romeo and Juliet, Anthony and Cleopatra, Benedict and Beatrice. C'mon! Play this scene like your relationship and future happiness depend on it!

THE ADRENALINE MOMENT

Scientists have discovered why we remember some things and not others. You will, for example, remember the first time you made love, but you are unlikely to remember what you ate for breakfast the day before yesterday. The reason for this is that, when something important happens to us, our brain becomes bathed with adrenaline, in effect putting a bookmark there. Nature is saying, "Remember this! It is important!" You can use this fact of nature in your acting by making a particular scene into an adrenaline moment. In other words, instead of playing it as a work-a-day event, make it a moment you will remember when you turn eighty-five years old and look back on your life.

★ The audience does not want to see characters get along. It wants to see them get it on!

★ These characters are the kind of thieves who go to jail for robbing a store of fifty dollars. They (you) are the very definition of small-timers. The way to play that is to raise the stakes. The circumstances of the play are that you want to steal a coin collection. Play it as if you are making plans to break into the White House. Make it Shakespearean in importance.

EMOTIONS

★ Psychologists recognize six basic human emotions: Happiness, surprise, fear, anger, disgust, and sadness. There is some disagreement about contempt being an emotion, but it equates to an air of superiority.

★ Thinking tends to lead to conclusions. Emotion tends to lead to action. Actors operate in an arena of emotion.

★ Frankly, the audience doesn't much care about the information in a scene. We empathize with emotion and put up with the information in order to get to the emotion.

★ Your character is objecting to her friend getting involved with an older man. You say to her, "When you're thirty-four, he'll be sixty-three!" You need to make that a bigger deal, like anybody who fools around with that kind of romantic age span is a candidate for a write up in the *Enquirer*.

★ Acting isn't about exchanging information with one another on stage. It is about exchanging emotion.

★ There is music to a scene. There are emotional builds, sudden drops into silence, and pauses. If you can't find the music, the scene will deliver information but will just lie there emotionally.

★ Acting choices that do not stimulate you emotionally are wasted acting choices.

THE BEN CASEY SCHOOL OF ACTING

Years ago there was a doctor show on TV called *Ben Casey*. I forget the actor who played the title role, but the fellow had only a single expression for everything. If he was happy he looked troubled; if he was mad he looked troubled; if he was attracted to a woman he looked troubled. It was so noticeable that he became a joke within acting classes. A teacher would say to an unexpressive student, "You are heading toward the Ben Casey school of acting."

★ Emotions do not themselves have any theatrical value. The fact that you can turn yourself into an emotional whirligig on stage is neither here nor there. You need to take some of that wonderful energy and refocus it into actions and objectives. Try to find some grace in your character.

★ You say you're going to marry a man named David, right? Well, that isn't just information like you might give the social security administration! You are going to be Mrs. David! That's better than being Mrs. Cletus or Mrs. Vern, isn't it? Are you proud of this guy? Are you tickled pink to be marrying a guy named David? Well, let us know that! You ever hear that song from *West Side Story* about a girl named Maria? "I just met a girl named...Ma-reee-ahhh!" Make the name special!

★ New actors are frequently too text-oriented. They want to learn the lines quickly and then start acting them in a naturalistic way. The truth is that acting has almost nothing to do with lines or words. And anyway, even when you *do* get to the words, the audience is more interested in how you *feel* about what you are saying than they are in the information itself.

★ Damn, you sound clinical! You sound like a doctor! Let your emotions speak.

★ I know you are feeling tense and angry today. It shows in your face. But you can't let your distress color the character so much. Try this: Fifteen minutes before your performance, go into the bathroom and grin at your silly self in the mirror. Don't rehearse lines, just grin. Medical science has proven that, if you behave a certain way, it will cause you to actually feel that way. Smiling and grinning at yourself releases endorphins into your system, a kind of natural narcotic.

ANGER

★ When you have a scene in which you must be angry, try looking under the mad to find the sad. There is frequently an element of hurt underneath the expression of anger.

★ Anger is self-fulfilling. A person who is angry will tend to filter out input that doesn't justify continuing to be angry. She won't want to listen to reason. An angry person is not likely to stop mid-scream and say, "Hey wait, this emotion is inappropriate." She needs to calm down first.

★ Imagine one male German shepherd going after another. That's anger. Or it for sure looks like it.

EXPRESSING ANGER

Anger is a fearsome emotion. When you were a child, you might well have been admonished or even punished for expressing your anger. If you have developed a pattern of not expressing anger, it will surely give you problems as an actor. You will, probably sooner rather than later, have to portray a character who is a hot head or is overtly angry. If you personally block anger in your life, you will have difficulty accessing it when you must use it in your art. Some scene study workshops are an okay place for making baby-steps in the expression of anger, but I don't think that acting class ought to be a substitute for therapy. An acting teacher may be sensitive and insightful, but she may not be qualified to deal with these kinds of deep-rooted psychological blocks. My advice to you is that, if you have trouble with the expression of anger, consider spending some time with a good therapist. In your head, write it off as acting lessons if you want to, but you really do need to address it.

EMOTIONAL EXPERIENCE

★ Joy and pain are on a moving spectrum. If you block your vulnerability so that you cannot be hurt, you simultaneously and unwittingly block a proportionate degree of your ability to experience joy. Shut down one, and you shut down the other. Actors need the full range of emotions in order to do their work. My recommendation is that you address the reasons for your narrow emotional range. You may not be able to do it alone. It may require the help of a good psychotherapist.

★ Be 100 percent of who you are. Wear it on your sleeve so the world can see it. Some will like it and some will not, but you will be authentic.

BEING IN TOUCH WITH YOUR EMOTIONS

If an actor lacks access to his emotions, he will have trouble acting—it's as simple as that. If he is out of touch with his own emotions, then he ought to work that out in therapy. An acting class is where you learn acting as an art form. While it is therapeutic and liberating to act, it is also true that acting workshops ought not to be a substitute for psychotherapy.

Not too long ago one of my Chicago students told me that he had never been angry enough to hit another person. That is, of course, not true. We have all been angry enough to hit someone. If he clings to that false notion, he will damage himself as an actor.

I remember a young actress I taught in Los Angeles who claimed never to have experienced profound love. She had the quickest smile and whitest teeth I have ever seen, and she was extremely intelligent. She also turned out to be anorexic and almost died not too long after she told me about not feeling love. Her issues went way beyond anything that an acting teacher should touch.

Emotions are automatic value responses. One person may be afraid of a mouse, while the next person is not. One person will be terrified of walking on a dark street at night, and the next person will not. One person may be delighted by the Christmas season, and the next person may approach it with foreboding. It is a factor of values. Emotions do not hover in space in a causeless manner. Emotion is connected to reason like the thighbone is to the hipbone. Emotions go off all the time. They are common currency for us humans. An actor needs to be in touch with his own feelings and those of the character. You may be portraying a character who is woefully out of touch with her emotions, but you can't do her justice unless you can access your own emotions.

★ Your emotions are a factor of your value system. In fact, you can define emotions as automatic value responses. For example, if I hold a live rat up by the tail and show it to five different people, I will likely get five different emotional responses. Somebody will think it is a cute critter and want to hold it, and someone else will run screaming from the room. Every character you play has her own set of values.

ACTING WITH THE HEART

★ You are too analytical. You're approaching acting like you might approach filling out an application for a second mortgage. Act with your heart, not your head! You know how you feel when you listen to music? Acting is more like that. Forget about the individual notes and just groove.

★ When I was a new actor, the note I got from my teachers most often was that I was "thinking too much." Back then I didn't understand this note very well. In my view, thinking was what we humans do. How could a character not think? It took me some years to deeply understand the connections between emotions and actions in an actor's art. My teachers were correct, but I wasn't ready at that point to hear them.

★ You learn acting through feeling and doing, like learning how to ride a bicycle. You don't learn it in a cerebral way. We can sit here and talk acting theory all night long and nobody in the room will be a much better actor than he was when he arrived.

> "The actor is an athlete of the heart."
> Antonin Artaud

★ You just told your best friend that you're in love with this younger guy. Act with expectation. How do you expect her to react to that news? You're delivering the line right now like a driving instructor telling a student to change lanes. Bo-o-o-r-r-i-n-g. If you don't care that you're in love, the audience won't care either.

★ When was the first time you told someone you love them? Those words don't come out of a person's mouth easily the first time as a rule. Yet here in the scene you're telling her you love her like you would tell her you prefer lace-up shoes.

★ Your character is how old? Forty-something? And you're dating a guy who is teaching you to roller-blade? Well, you sound like you are announcing that he's teaching you to knit! The whole point of the line is that this new romance makes you feel like a kid again. The audience wants to know how you feel. Act with your heart!

LOSS OF CONTROL

★ Your emotions are controlling you. You can hardly be understood through all that sobbing, and you appear to be genuinely distraught. It's marvelous that you can stimulate yourself emotionally like that, but your emotion is only part of the theatrical equation. If you are out of control emotionally on stage, it will make your audience nervous and will cost them their suspension of disbelief. Loss of control is a violation of the implied theatrical contract.

★ Did you ever feel an inappropriate urge and not act on it? Maybe you feel an urge to kiss somebody or jump off a balcony or laugh in church? That is a good example of your emotions going one way and your thinking another.

BEING IN THE MOMENT

★ What does it mean to "be in the moment"? I think it means you need to surprise yourself.

DIDEROT'S PARADOX

A century ago, philosopher Denis Diderot wrote a famous treatise entitled "The Paradox of the Actor" in which he asserted that no matter how much an actor tries, he can never be 100 percent "in the moment." If he succeeded, blocking out all other conscious considerations, he might just wander off the stage or maybe hurt somebody in the big murder scene. Diderot correctly pointed out that an actor must always have a controlling distance from his performance. Indeed, the audience requires that the actor be in control of his performance! If the actor appears out of control on stage, it makes the audience nervous.

★ One of the most difficult aspects of acting is learning how not to anticipate. Acting is, after all, a process of learning lines and then repeating them, yes? If you know that, in a moment, someone is going to come crashing through the front window, it is like sitting on the train tracks watching a train approach. You begin to tense up before anything happens, and that is an acting error. The goal is to be in the present moment. You're not in the present moment if even a small part of your brain is thinking about what is coming in the next scene. The way you pull off this hat trick is to play an action 100 percent. Put your mind totally into playing the present action and you will be as much "in the moment" as it is possible for you to be. You will trick yourself into being surprised when the other actor comes crashing through the window.

★ Rehearsal is a funny thing. You work out the scene, then once you have it the way you want it, you have to forget all of that. When the curtain goes up in front of an audience, you must trick your brain into not remembering all that good stuff you did in rehearsal. You have to play the scene as if it had never before been rehearsed and as if you have no idea what is coming next.

★ You look like you are trying to remember your lines rather than playing the scene. The audience isn't much interested in watching you do that. Acting is doing. If you are trying to remember lines, then *that* is what you are doing.

★ Acting choices never become automated. Just because your choices worked magic at yesterday's run-through, doesn't mean it will happen again today. Acting is an art that happens in the present moment. It's not like, say, sculpture, where you can work on a bust for a while and then toss a damp rag over it until tomorrow. With acting, every time you finish a scene or an act or a whole play, it is like you destroy the bust. Tomorrow, you have to start all over again from scratch with fresh clay.

BEGINNING IN THE MIDDLE

★ Scenes begin in the middle, not at the beginning. When you knock on the apartment door, you intend to reconcile with your husband. That is the objective. But what was going on with you before you knocked on that door? How long were you standing outside working up your nerve? How badly do you need a drink and how can you cover that need? Is your hair combed? What happens if your husband has another woman visiting him. It has after all been a year since you have seen him. From the audience's perspective, this scene begins when he goes to the door in response to your knock. From your perspective it begins probably en route to the apartment. And by the way, what is the temperature outside? I notice you're not wearing a jacket. It is midnight, yes?

JUSTIFYING

★ You must justify everything on stage, including the impulse to tell a story. You're pretty believable within the telling, but it isn't credible that you would have told the story in the first place. The acting error is not happening at the moment of the speech. It is happening much earlier, before the audience discovers you in the bar at opening curtain. Let's examine it: This play (*Danny and the Deep Blue Sea* by John Patrick Shanley) is rough stuff. Your character meets this guy in a bar and within five minutes is telling him about how her father sexually abused her. Now, think about this for a minute: In real time, five minutes is awfully quick for one person to be telling another such an intimate story. Right? That suggests to me that the topic is gnawing at you as the curtain rises. You don't tell him that off the cuff. Emotionally, you need to be like a loaded gun with a hair trigger. It shouldn't take very much to set you off, to launch you into the story.

★ You don't have to know what you are going to be doing for the entire scene. The circumstances will take care of all that. All you have to do is get yourself on stage. You need a reason for entering the scene. After that, you play moment to moment, action to action. Surprise yourself!

★ In this scene, the writer has you state specifically and honestly the nature of your relationship with your best friend. You tell her

that you are in fact a ditz, and she is Miss Perfect, a characterization that your character can be pretty sure is going to offend
her. Now in life it is not likely that one would be that candid or
incisive. We all play roles with our friends to some degree, but
we don't generally spell them out. That means you have to justify doing something extraordinary. You can't just tell her you're
the ditz and she's Miss Perfect and all is right with the world.
When you tell her these things, there is a chance she will object
or get angry or deny it or something maybe even worse. There
is a risk involved!

MULTITASKING

★ Most people can do two things at the same time. What is your
primary job now that you've pitched camp for the night? Make
a fire, cook some dinner, relax a little. The conversation with
Lenny is something you do while you are doing those other
things. Right now, it looks like you came to this place along
the riverbank just so you could sit down and talk to Lenny
man to man.

LAUGHTER

★ It's almost impossible to fake laughter. Laughter is most often a
factor of mood. I can't think of anything that sounds more fake
than a fake laugh.

★ Probably the reason your laughter in the scene sounds so fake
right now is that you are personally nervous. Your character is
not nervous, you are. The correction to this problem is in relaxation. You have to allow the character to impose herself on you
instead of the other way around.

★ People laugh for a lot of reasons, not just because something is funny. Laughter is one of those "I'm OK, you're OK" things. Scientists liken it to the way that monkeys groom one another.

★ Nervous actors will tend to force laughter and it just sounds fake, thereby hurting their case in audition or jarring the audience in actual performance. My advice is if the script calls for a vocal laugh but the moment is not motivated, it may be best to do something other than laugh.

COMEDY

★ Stop trying to be funny. Comedy is drama heightened, enriched, and oxygenated. Find what is true in the scene rather than what is funny. Then raise the stakes. The most brilliant comic actor in history was Charlie Chaplin. Study him.

★ Okay, the deal with this scene is that you climb on top of him and mislead him into thinking you are ready for sex. Then as soon as he's turned on, you roll over and say goodnight. The thing is that you don't look like you're actually ready for sex. There is a distance you are keeping from him. Even if it isn't true, play the part of the woman who is surrendering to his overwhelming masculinity and charm. You just can't help yourself! Men love that stuff, and most often they even believe it. Then as soon as you get him going, roll off and say good night. Leave him lying there. It'll guarantee a big laugh.

★ When you enter the apartment, she's already pissed. Why? Because you went to a wedding with her, caught the bridal bouquet yourself, and threw it back. To you, it was a sort of cute moment. It made the guys laugh. To her, it was the beginning of the end for your relationship. Men and women can look at the same situation in completely different ways. Remember that book by John Gray, *Men Are from Mars, Women Are from Venus?* There's a lot of truth in that title, as well as a heck of a lot of potential for comedy.

> Lift the hood of any good comedy and you will find a good drama.

★ Make sure you deliver your comedy punch lines very clearly. Don't rush them. In this scene, the other actor says to you, "You have slept with two and a half men," and you respond by saying, "You leave Jerry Potts out of this!" That's funny stuff. It makes the audience imagine what might be the situation with Jerry Potts. Therefore, Jerry Potts needs to be a very specific image in your head and reference. You should know what his situation is even if the line doesn't spell it out. The audience can tell by your reaction whether or not Jerry Potts is an actual person. The joke works best if he is real.

★ The idea in *Murder at the Howard Johnson's* is that the three characters are all plotting murder at one time or another. The comedy is in the fact that none of them are murderers. They are regular, nice, neurotic people. You have to play it for real. Neither you nor I are really murderers, right? So if we decided to murder somebody, we'd probably make a mess of it. There is a heck of a lot of comedic potential in that set up.

★ *Waiting for Godot* can be the most tedious play in the world if you don't get humor into it. I think how funny it would be if it were Ralph Kramden and Ed Norton who were waiting for Godot.

CRYING

★ If you have to cry in a scene, the acting trick is to try not to cry. We humans do not easily share our emotions with one another. If we feel like we're going to cry, we often try to stifle the impulse.

★ Twist your face into a mask of grief and you will feel an impulse to cry. Then resist the impulse.

HOLDING BACK THE TEARS

While Joe Namath was a star quarterback for the New York Jets, he also had a financial stake in a Manhattan restaurant and nightclub. When Mafia types started hanging out at the club, the NFL decided the image was bad for football and told Namath that he must sell his interest in the club or resign from football. (Now mind you Namath was just about the hottest player in the entire league at the time.) Well, Namath decided he would resign rather than be dictated to this way. He called a press conference. The table at which he sat was crowded with microphones, and TV news cameras were choked together in front of him. He began to announce his retirement and, before he could get through two sentences, he began to cry. Then he wiped his eyes, laughed at himself for crying, and started again. Once again he started crying, and once again he wiped his eyes, laughed, and started over. It went on like this for several false starts, and I sat at home watching with fascination.

This was an early lesson for me about how to cry on cue. Joe Namath was a big strong man for whom tears were a sign of weakness. He would cry, then laugh; cry, then laugh. I saw right then that the trick to crying was to try not to cry.

★ New actors are always worrying about how to make themselves cry, and it is such a waste of time. In the first place, pain is not always accompanied by actual liquid tears. In the second place, we humans are usually not too eager to share our emotions with others, not even those who are closest to us. Therefore, if we start to cry, we are most likely to try to stifle it. In other words, if you want to cry, try not to cry.

★ Why do people cry at weddings? Because a wedding is both the joyous beginning of a relationship with a partner and the sad end of a child-adult relationship with a parent.

LAUGHING THROUGH THE TEARS

Often, we humans laugh at things that hurt too much. We can't handle the pain with tears, so we laugh. When President John Kennedy was assassinated, I was in the Air Force stationed at Andrews Air Force Base in Washington, D.C. It was to that airport that his body was returned from Dallas, Texas, where he had been killed. When word of the assassination came in, all flights were grounded, and I was stuck right there at the very spot where the Presidential party would arrive. Between the time of his death and the time his body arrived at Andrews AFB, I heard the first "dead Kennedy" joke. I later heard it repeated in other places, but I know for a fact that it was made up right there, by a soldier. The joke was: "What is Jackie bringing back from Dallas?" Answer: "A Jack in the Box." Tasteless? You bet it was. But there is a huge acting lesson there. Soldiers in particular were hurt by the untimely death of the Commander in Chief. And soldiers are mostly big manly men who do not cry. When all of that emotion and pain came together, it was expressed as humor.

WORKING WITH OPPOSITES

★ Try working with opposites. If a line is written to be yelled, say it quietly. If the scene involves tears, see what happens when you mix laughter with the tears.

THE AUDIENCE

★ The audience is not a lurker. It is your storytelling partner. It has a function and a role in the theatrical transaction, and that is true whether you are doing a play or a movie. The point of acting is to tell a story to the audience. The roots of acting are in shamanism, pre-Christian religious practices. When you act you call the tribe together. When they get there, you had better have more to show them than that you have the ability to be honest and truthful.

★ Who are you talking to? Shakespeare's soliloquies frequently work best if they are directed to a restive audience. If you don't do that, you are faced with the task of standing on stage and talking to yourself for a minute and a half. When was the last time you talked out loud to yourself for a minute and a half?

> There is an old theater maxim that is often
> true and always worth keeping in mind:
> Plays are written for adults and played for children.

★ In moments of intimacy and intensity, you tend to physically close in on the other actor and to speak with quiet urgency. As a matter of communication, that's not unilaterally a bad idea. The problem is that when you close in like that and get so quiet, you are not projecting enough volume so that the audience can hear the dialogue. You must never forget that the actor is there primarily for the benefit of the audience members. You must never ever exclude them from your theatrical moment. I remember being told by my high school acting teacher that I should act for the deaf lady in the back row. That's actually not bad advice!

★ Young kids in school productions are generally advised to "open up" to the audience, to "face downstage." Professional actors learn how to accomplish the same effect without always physically facing the audience. I once heard someone say of the late actress Geraldine Page that "she could do more acting with her back than most actors can do with their front." As long as you are aware of and include the audience members, you do not need to face them all the time.

★ Think of the audience as a congregation. Take to the stage the way a priest takes to the pulpit.

★ Bring the audience to you. Don't chase them.

★ Stop bending over from the waist during moments of intense communication! If you go to any high school play, you'll see the kids doing that. They'll have a line like, "I love you!" and they'll bend at the waist and sprawl their arms out, hoping the extra movement will enhance the voltage. The reason you tend to bend over like that is that you don't trust the words or your intention. Stand up! Be a magnet.

★ If you feel that the audience is shifting around in their seats and has become distracted, the correction is to stop. Do not go faster or speak louder. Just stop. Say nothing. Reconnect with the moment and your intention. The audience will return in a heartbeat.

★ The connection between you and the audience is sort of like a radio station signal. You want to make sure you are not slightly off the dial indicator. Your signal should be clean, open, and direct. You want the audience to tune in to you easily.

TRUTHFULNESS

Not long ago, a young woman audited my Chicago acting class. During the break she followed me to the coffee machine. I could tell she was less than enchanted for some reason, and so I asked her what was up. "To me," she explained, "the point of acting is to be truthful." I poured ground coffee into the paper filter and acknowledged her point. "I agree with that. Truthful is good. But what about the audience?" "What do you mean?" she asked. "What are they doing while you're being truthful? Do you figure they came to the theater to see you be truthful?" "Well, I think they expect truthful acting." "Yes, I agree. But what is the difference between being truthful in the theater and being truthful at the grocery store or shopping mall?" She looked perplexed. I poured the water in the top of the coffee machine and turned my attention fully to her. "If honesty and truthfulness were the main focus of the audience, they could get that without paying for a theater ticket. Heck, they probably could have stayed home and seen some honesty and truthfulness, don't you think?"

★ Why do you keep hiding from the audience? Do you realize you're doing that? You're speaking through clenched teeth and turning upstage too often. We want to see and hear you! The reason you act is to communicate with an audience.

★ Embrace the audience. Be available to them. Actors lead and audiences follow. You can't hide on stage.

★ Never underestimate the intelligence of your audience.

★ The idea is to establish in the audience a sense of empathy (Brecht excepted).

GETTING BENEATH THE LITERAL

★ Director Mike Nichols says that when he directs a scene, he tries to find out what the scene is really about. That is good advice. Get underneath the obvious and literal level of the scene. Haven't you ever had the experience of talking to someone about a movie or the weather or a book when, underneath it all, you're really thinking about how much you'd like to kiss her?

★ On the surface, this scene is about two guys who are one-upping one another about their respective knowledge of the career of Maria Callas. The audience is not going to put out good money to learn a bunch of facts about Maria Callas though. They can go to the library and read up on her for free. They want to know about the relationship between you two, how you feel about things. Why are you putting so much of your lonely energy into Maria Callas trivia? What is the scene *really* about?

★ When the other character enters the scene, your character says, "I'm glad to see you," but that's a lie. You can't take lines in a script to be literal.

★ You told your friend that you are having an affair with someone at the office. She asked you if the sex was good. You replied, "I guess so." What the heck does that mean? Is it good or not? If it is not good, why on earth are you doing it? Just because the line expresses ambivalence, that does not mean you are in fact ambivalent. It could also mean that you don't want to admit to your friend that you are having bone-rattling, knee-buckling wonderful sex at lunchtime.

★ In life, the words we say are very frequently not at all what we really mean or feel. When you say to your scene partner, "I'm glad to meet you," that doesn't mean that you really are. He could be setting your teeth on edge, and you might still say the same words. How often have you said "good morning," and not really felt it was a good morning at all?

★ In this scene, you are playing a college professor who is accused of sexual harassment. We in the audience saw the earlier scene in which you put your arms around her when she was distraught. The fact is that you did indeed do the things she is now accusing you of. You did indeed touch her, and you did indeed offer to work with her privately and to give her a passing grade. So, here is your acting choice: Did you feel any attraction to her? I realize the dialogue has you professing total innocence, but that may be a lie. Frankly, if it were me playing that role, I would allow the attraction in the hope that it would evoke a feeling of shame and embarrassment, which would give me more to work with acting-wise.

★ Damien, you are telling him that the strange substance in that dish is "nun shit." What kind of acting choice are you making there? Are you taking that literally? I doubt seriously it is actually nun shit. I mean, where on earth would you get a dish of nun shit? I'm willing to bet that this is either dog shit or your own shit. Your plan is that if he thinks it is nun shit, it will make it more palatable to him. When you tell him it's nun shit, smile reassuringly.

RELATING TO YOUR SCENE PARTNER

★ Acting is about reaching out and touching somebody. It's not about communicating with yourself. Put your focus on the other guy in the scene.

★ Actors working together in a scene should be as responsive to one another as lovers. That is why, when I give notes on scenes, I sometimes give adjustments to Actor Number One when I am really trying to help Actor Number Two.

★ The great actors in history have been generous. By that, I mean they put a lot of their energy into their scene partners, not themselves. Vanessa Redgrave, Anthony Hopkins, Robert De Niro, Dustin Hoffman... These are all very generous actors. I believe that acting should be approached with humility, not arrogance.

★ The reason you are worried about losing control is that you are too focused on your own self. Acting is sudden, and it radiates outward. Sort of like if you saw a child run in front of a car and you sprang to save her.

★ Your scene partner is not a china doll. She can take care of herself. I feel like you are holding back with her. You'll actually do her a favor if you play the scene full out. She'll have more to react to.

★ There can be real power on stage when you maintain a distance from the other character. The normal impulse is to keep closing in on her, but try staying all the way on the other side of the stage and see what happens.

BE UNPREDICTABLE

One of the most valuable gifts you can give your fellow actor on stage is to be unpredictable. Even though she may know what is coming up because the two of you have rehearsed the scene forever, you still should not be predictable. Don't let her know precisely where you are going.

I have never had the privilege of acting with Robert De Niro, but I have friends who have, and they tell me that this is one of his strongest qualities. You'll be doing a scene with him and even though he's saying the words in the script, you have the feeling that he is just about to go off someplace else. What this does is keep you riveted, and it makes *you* look good! It is an old and reliable maxim that it is always better to act with strong actors, because they automatically strengthen your performance.

Please do not misunderstand me. I'm not suggesting that you play games with the script or with your intent. Nor am I suggesting that you not do what you rehearsed. The point is that, in life, we continually have choices. As I write these words, I could very easily switch and start writing a letter to the editor of the *New York Times* or an entry in my diary. But I don't do that because I am committed to what I am saying to you. The possibility exists though, and that is the important thing. A new actor tends to learn the lines, commit them firmly to memory, work out the actions and objectives—and that is the end of it. As he plays his scene, he forgets that the character continually has options. In his mind, there are no options, because he has memorized the scene as it is supposed to unfold. You see?

Shakespeare advised that an actor "hold the mirror up to nature." In nature, we have choices all of our waking life. And so, too, should it be with your characters. To play it that way is to give a gift to your scene partner.

★ Acting is based largely on trust. You must let your scene partner know that it is okay for him to be honest, even if that honesty might offend. The problem I'm having with you two is that you are dealing with one another as if you just met at a coffee shop rather than as two people who have made three babies so far. I feel like you are worried about offending one another. You can't act that way.

★ Stop pawing her. Try to attract her. Be a desirable target. Get her to walk into *your* arms.

★ When you act, it is necessary to have a for-real effect on your scene partner. If you don't, you're just playing with yourself.

★ Deal with the reality of your scene partner. When you look at her, you will not see a character. You will see the actress! Acting is not about hallucinating a character.

★ Go ahead and stick your tongue in his ear. It's nothing personal.

★ Oh come on, she's your wife! It's perfectly feasible that you might slap her bottom. Work it out with your scene partner in rehearsal. This kind of thing isn't really personal like it is in real life. Now, if you leave the theater and smack her bottom out on the street, she would be perfectly correct to knock your block off. Bottom slapping, like kissing and the rest of it, is professional behavior in the theater.

★ The given relationship between the two of you is that you are friends, but your relationship still seems static to me. Suppose you act as though you are sisters? The audience would never know, and it would warm up the scene. People who are friends or lovers relate to one another in familiar shorthand. You finish each other's sentences, anticipate jokes, rejoice in shared values.

TAKING RISKS

★ Make acting choices that may get you into trouble.

★ When acting is right, it feels risky, like walking a high wire without a safety net or like taking your clothes off in public. The growth of an actor is in finding the exhilaration in that feeling. I too often see beginning actors pull back from it.

★ Milk is homogenized and pasteurized. Actors are not. Actors are best when they are raw, unfiltered, a little dangerous.

★ If you feel like you should do something on stage, there is a very good likelihood that you should, even if you didn't rehearse it like that or it might be surprising behavior for your character. You get into trouble when you censor and edit yourself. It is almost always better to be risky and trust your impulses, even if you are uncertain about why you have a particular impulse.

★ Imagine that acting has a campfire at its center. All you're doing is warming your hands and cooking a marshmallow. I want to see you jump over the thing, risking a butt burn or something. Your acting is too safe!

> Acting is more like playing in a sandbox than a shoe box. You have more room to move around, and it's okay to kick some sand in the other actor's face from time to time.

★ You're blocking your emotions in an unusual way, by habitually using a kind of halting phrasing. Note how you take a single sentence and break it up into four or five sentences with pauses in between the short phrases? You don't do that in life. Every one of those pauses is like a tent stake in the ground. You're anchoring yourself, controlling things. It will feel more dangerous if you just say the whole sentence straight out, but that will be better for you emotionally. An audience doesn't want to sit there and watch you be a control freak. You are pursuing the wrong goal. Good acting will never ever feel safe, no matter how slow you go. Good acting is risky and a little scary.

SWING THE CAT

Like a lot of artistic geniuses, Marlon Brando has often explained his technique in terms that others might find a little bewildering. I remember one of his directors saying in an interview that he was perplexed when Brando showed up for a preproduction meeting and explained that he wanted to play his character like a loaf of bread. Several years ago, actor Edward Norton was appearing on *The Tonight Show* to promote *The Score,* a movie in which he co-starred with Robert De Niro and Marlon Brando. He laughed when he told Jay Leno about the time on the set when Brando bridled at too-close direction. He reportedly told the director, "Hey, I have to have room to swing the cat." I understand that expression to mean that he did not want to set his performance too tightly—and he wanted the director to leave him alone about it. He preferred to surprise himself and his scene partner. After all, swinging a cat is likely to get you scratched big time, but it is probably exciting to watch. Maybe one day somebody will write a book of humorous Brando-isms, similar to Yogi-isms.

★ We know that you two have been in bed all afternoon, right? And we know that, while he did the post-coital snooze, it started snowing in New York. Several inches have accumulated according to the script. So, when you tell him that he isn't going to get very far in all that snow in his Gucci loafers, try helping him take his pants back off. I realize there is nothing in the script that tells you to do that, but it doesn't matter. He's not going to let you take them off anyway. But it makes sense that, if you have a half a foot of snow outside and he can't leave anyway, maybe the two of you would have some more delicious sex.

★ Don't be afraid to be corny. We are corny in life. We make bad jokes, break into out-of-tune songs, and do awful imitations of Jerry Lewis and Groucho Marx and Mae West. This is the stuff of relationships, daily life. The playwright isn't likely to tell you to imitate Mae West on that line, but your character might think to do it anyway. Do it! You're not betraying the playwright. You're just having fun.

CREATING ATMOSPHERE

★ If you want it to appear that you are looking at something, then actually look at something rather than pretend to look at something. When you pretend to look out the window in that scene, you should focus on some actual distant point here in the studio. Like the light switch or that painting over there. If you want the effect to be that you are looking far into the distance, then look at a smaller thing on the wall, like that nail sticking out of the wall or that piece of brick. The same principle applies to what you hear. If you want to appear to be hearing something, then actually listen for something. Do you hear the fire engine a block away? Do you hear some people laughing on the sidewalk outside?

★ A garage has a different atmosphere than a cafeteria. An airplane has a different atmosphere than the cab of a truck. Even a poker game has its own unique atmosphere. Atmosphere affects how you feel.

★ You're talking to the troops in this piece, Joe. Outside! In the winter! Without a microphone! Yet you look like you're having a quiet chat with some friends on the beach. There is nothing intimate or small about this speech. Also, when you are speaking outdoors to a lot of people, there is a compensating higher pitch to your voice that counterbalances the way sound travels outside.

★ It's Christmas, darlin'. In New Jersey. Wear a coat.

★ The action in *A Hatful of Rain* takes place during baseball season. There are references made to that fact. So why are you not dressed for summer? You have not used the baseball season reference to your advantage. The season ranges from summer into fall, yes? Well, why not decide it is mid-summer rather than early fall? In the deep heat of summer, especially in New York, it is humid and still. You'll wear fewer clothes. A quiet fan might be running in the corner. It's sweaty, and sweaty equates to sensual. Heat makes you move more slowly. You two are supposed to be inappropriately attracted to one another. Do yourselves a favor and strip down a bit. Slow down the action. Take time to breathe and to perspire a bit. Be aware of one another's bodies. It's summer.

★ This play takes place in the Deep South where it is hot and humid—rumpled, dampened bedsheets and all that. This will affect your rhythm. Your rhythm is so quick you could be doing this thing in an igloo. Michael Chekhov had much wisdom to share about the importance of atmosphere in a scene. Get his book *On the Technique of Acting* (Harper Collins, 1991).

★ Consider your environment. It is dusk in the summer. Crickets can be heard in the bushes. Maybe distant field hands can be heard calling to one another. Your voice carries differently in the stillness of dusk than it does at noon, know what I mean?

WAYS OF PRETENDING

You will hear a lot of terms thrown around in acting class. Sense memory, emotional recall, endowment, and affective memory are just a few. In my classes, I don't like to use a whole lot of terms because I think they invite an overly analytical approach to acting. Some acting teachers even make up a bunch of their own terms! It is bewildering and can get in the way of good acting. What it really all boils down to anyway is pretending. For example, you "endow" a glass of water with the properties of whisky. It burns when it goes down your throat. Now you endow the same glass of water with the properties of a Coca-Cola. The carbonation causes an effect in your mouth. Now endow the glass of water with the properties of hot tea. You don't gulp it down, you sip it—and so on. Children play these kinds of pretending games all the time.

Stanislavsky is the one who made up the term "affective memory," borrowing the basic idea from French psychologist Theodule Ribot (1839–1916). Ribot's observation was that a person can recall a distant past emotion if he recalls the physical sensations associated with it. This is what is at the root of "emotional recall" and "sense memory," terms that were made popular by Lee Strasberg. If you are playing a scene that takes place on a moonlit beach, you would recall a moonlit beach from your past. How does the breeze feel against your arms? Is the air warm or is there a chill? What sound does the surf make? Can you see any ships on the horizon? Are you barefoot? How does the wet sand feel between your toes? Again, it is pretending. All of acting is pretending. Don't get bogged down in all the terms.

★ There is a Christmas tree in your friend's living room. My question for you is, when do you first see the tree? I'll bet you saw that tree the moment you stepped into the room, but right now you seem not to be aware of it until you are two feet away. You don't need to wait until you get to the tree to acknowledge that you saw it.

★ Your character just walked ten miles in the hot southern sun. You asked for a drink of water, which is logical enough. How about if you also dipped your fingers into that glass of water and rubbed it on your forehead? You can cool yourself off in more ways than one.

★ When you say that the sun feels great, be like a cat. Stretch a little, purr a little. Experience the warm sunshine with your whole body.

SUBSTITUTION

★ You are in a scene in which you are supposed to be shocked by something. Maybe the scene is not shocking you no matter how much you pretend. Try getting in touch with a time you were really shocked, like maybe when you walked in on your parents doing the wild thing. Then, knowing what that shocked feeling is, you go back to the text. Next time you play it, the correct feeling should start coming in naturally. If it still doesn't work, use a different and more powerful substitution.

BEING SPECIFIC

★ Make every single reference specific. When you say to your scene partner, "Remember Anne Fishback?" you need to know precisely and specifically who Anne Fishback was. If the script doesn't tell you, then make it up.

LEE STRASBERG'S FRUIT SALAD

Don't be afraid of the fruit salad. I first learned about it from an old documentary about Lee Strasberg at the Actors Studio. After watching two actors present a scene, Lee waited for everybody in the theater to settle down and then quietly asked the actress if she knew how to make a fruit salad. She of course didn't have any idea what he was talking about since fruit salads were not relevant to her scene. She glanced nervously at the packed theater and asked Lee what exactly he had in mind. "Do you know how to make a fruit salad?" he asked again, more insistently. "Yes, I do." "How do you do it?" "You want me to tell you right now how I make a fruit salad?" "Yes." "Well, I cut up some strawberries and put in some other fruit..." "What kind of fruit? I want you to tell me precisely how you make a fruit salad, step by step." "I peel a banana and chop it into the bowl. Then I cut up some grapes..." On and on the fruit salad recipe went. When she finished, Strasberg said, "Yes, and after you do all of those things, you have a fruit salad. You can't have a fruit salad until you do all those things." He then explained to her that as an actor she was trying to have a fruit salad before she had done all those things. He pointed out that there are a whole lot of individual and distinct thoughts that occur in between most verbalized communications. It is necessary for an actor to allow all of those thoughts to occur. Don't skip them and go straight to the line.

★ Your girlfriend told you that she feels guilty for having an office affair because, as she puts it, "You are only supposed to have sex to have babies." When you tell her that is silly, what are you referring to? Her guilt? Stupid church rules? Both? Be specific in your thinking.

★ Orient yourself to the auditorium. When you say something like, "Is that due north?," you should be referencing a particular direction in the theater auditorium itself. Or when you say, "Didn't the sofa used to be under the window?," you should know which wall has the window. It might be the downstage (nonexistent) wall. Or if you say something like "Is that a ship or a whale out there?," you should be orienting to a specific point in the room.

★ Your entrance line is, "What? What is it? I ordered the cake." You don't have to run all those words together. The line is comprised of at least three different and specific thoughts. "What?" (She doesn't answer you. After a beat, ask her again...) "What is it?" (Her silence is ominous and threatening. Lead her away from the subject of spousal abuse and onto something lighter...) "I ordered the cake."

★ When you have an incomplete or interrupted sentence, complete the thought in your head even if you don't verbalize it. If I say, for example, "Sally, was it you who...?" I need to have in my head what I started out to say: "Sally, was it you who threw that baby out the window?" I may be too astonished and shocked to finish the thought, but I need to know what the thought was that I was trying to express. It works the same way when the other actor interrupts you mid-sentence. You should have the whole thought in your head from the get-go.

★ You're cheating on your husband, and you're a good Catholic. Your line is, "I could go to hell for this," but you're acting like hell is Yosemite or Acapulco! A good Catholic is going to have a vivid picture of the hell awaiting a sinner. You ever read Dante's *Inferno?* He describes hell pretty clearly.

★ At one point in the scene, you pick up a rag doll that is presumably owned by your young daughter whom you have not seen for a year. You need to endow that rag doll with meaning. The doll is a stand-in for your daughter who you still cannot take into your embrace. Allow the rag doll to move you emotionally.

★ Where does that wad of money come from? Prostitution, right? The woman is a madam. There's no telling who has been touching this wad of money. Well, when it's time for you to throw it on the table in disgust, let it pass through your mind that it smells vaguely of Ortho-Gynol.

★ Lenny just handed you a dead mouse, guy! And you're holding the thing like you want to play hacky sack with it. Remember the plague from your history books? Mice played a large part in that.

CONFLICT

★ Unless you are playing a character, like the Stage Manager in *Our Town,* who is not directly involved in the action of the play, you will need to find the conflict your character is experiencing. There are only three kinds of possible conflict: conflict with yourself, conflict with another character, and conflict with the situation. At least one type of conflict needs to be in play 100 percent of the time when you are on stage. You can have more than one kind of conflict, but you can't have none. The presence of conflict is one of the defining characteristics of theatrical reality.

★ You're having difficulty with the acting principle, "conflict with the situation." You seem to understand "conflict with the other character" and "conflict with yourself," but "conflict with the situation" is giving you trouble. Remember when you came to my apartment recently? Remember how afraid you were of my daughter's dog, Nugs? That's "conflict with the situation." You couldn't negotiate with anybody, and yet there was a way you would win and a way you would lose, which are essential elements of any negotiation. You would win if Nugs did not bite you; you would lose if he did bite you. And so you acted the best way you knew how in order not to get bitten.

★ I notice that you frequently turn your back on your scene partner. Do you feel how the tension in the scene dissipates when you do that? It is okay to turn your back, but you want to always be moving toward conflict, not away from it. If you opt to physically turn away, make a simultaneous commitment to fill the moment emotionally.

★ While conflict is a vital element of a scene, it does not necessarily equate to a fistfight. You can be in conflict over whether to eat the cherry pie or the chocolate cake. You can be in conflict over which lover is getting on top tonight. You can be in conflict over whether to take your vacation in Rome or Paris. Instead of conflict, think more in terms of *obstacle*.

★ I understand and appreciate that the dialogue has you saying, "I want to get out of here!" But notice that the scene does not allow you to actually go anywhere even by its end. Therefore, you should be careful about making a false exit. Even if you are telling the other character that you don't want to be there, try telling him in a confrontational way rather than trying to run away. Invite the conflict! Move toward the conflict! Be very wary of making an acting choice that amounts to, "I don't want to be here." If you don't want to be in the scene, neither will the audience.

NEGOTIATING

★ Acting is not a process of your turn, my turn, your line, my line. It is a continual in-the-moment communication, like making love. When your scene partner is talking, you should be listening in an active way. Active listening means that even if you don't interrupt the person speaking, you are continually thinking of responses to what is being said to you. You are forming responses and then deciding not to express them, yet.

★ Playwright and director David Mamet thinks of scenes as negotiations. In any negotiation, there must be a way you can win and a way you can lose. Right now, you're just breezing in and informing your scene partner how it is. There seems to be no possibility that something he might say or do would cause you to have second thoughts. In other words, you are positioning yourself above the possibility of negotiation. I'd call that an acting error.

★ You guys are talking *at* each other! Remember, there is a difference between talking *at* and talking *with!* To me, if feels like you are sequentially orating. You'll correct that if you simply listen to one another.

PROJECTION

★ "Speak up!"

★ Project your whole essence, not just your voice, into the theater auditorium. Fill the place with your life force. Let us know that you believe in your heart that you deserve to be seen and heard.

★ Early in my acting career, I took a class with famed New York casting director Michael Shurtleff. (His book, *Audition* [Bantam, 1979], is still one of the best on the subject. I studied with him before he wrote it and was probably one of his guinea pigs.) I remember the day Shurtleff got frustrated with a young actor who was not projecting. He told the class that he wasn't going to give anybody projection notes any more because, "If an actor wants to be heard, then he will be. If he doesn't want to be heard, then he won't be an actor for long." It may sound harsh, but it is dead-on true. If your audience can't hear you, then what's the point?

VOICE

★ Make yelling a rare choice in acting. If there is any other way to express an emotion, choose the other way. Use yelling as sparingly as you would an exclamation point when you write a letter.

★ Stella, even at mid-day, is still post-coital. She and Stanley made the beast with two backs all night long. A post-coital person is a satisfied and relaxed person. A relaxed person's voice is going to shift into a lower register. Think pillow-talk.

BODY LANGUAGE

★ Smile! The human smile says, "I won't hurt you." It can be a valuable tool regardless of the content of the scene.

★ Go ahead and gesture! Use your hands and arms. They are extremely graceful and expressive. In evolution, humans gestured before they spoke words after all.

★ I have read several studies about gestures. One conclusion, for example, is that people who do not gesture have more trouble remembering things. Gesturing is natural to humans. Don't be afraid to do it.

★ Tighten up your ass cheeks when you deliver that speech. Doing so will cause everything you say to seem more important.

★ Put your knees together and sit up in the chair. You are playing a diplomat, not a lounge lizard!

ENJOYING YOURSELF

★ Where did you get the idea that acting is equivalent to suffering? It is a joy!

★ Why is it that so many professional actors stop having fun when they act? Don't you remember when you first acted in high school? Wasn't it fun? Well, it still *should* be that way. Your acting is efficient, and your technique is sound, but somewhere along the way you have lost your joy. Your acting has no soul. If the actor on stage is not enjoying the process of performing, I guarantee that the audience will not enjoy the actor's performance.

> "We artists and actors are lucky because we are held together by art, which in history-making times is even more necessary than ever to the inner life of the people."
> Constantin Stanislavsky (letter to Maxim Gorky, 1933)

SELF-MONITORING

★ If a scene is not working, you tend to step outside yourself and monitor your actions as you continue playing the scene. You become self-aware and self-critical. This is a terrible acting trap, because once you begin monitoring yourself, you are no longer thinking about the circumstances of the play. The way to correct a scene gone wrong is to refocus on what your character wants and to try putting your energies into the other actor in the scene.

★ You are too aware of your acting, like when a tennis player is too aware of his serve. I suggest you read a book entitled *The Inner Game of Tennis* by Timothy Gallwey (Random House, revised 1997), which talks about shifting your attention away from your serve and onto where you want the ball to be. This approach is actually key in all championship sports.

SWITCHING ACTIONS AND OBJECTIVES

★ This is an interesting transition. You're on the couch getting ready to make illicit love with your girlfriend when the phone rings. It is your ten-year-old daughter calling, and she needs daddy at home because her tooth fell out. The reason you are having trouble in that transitional moment is that, when you are on the sofa, you know what your objective is. When the phone rings, you just get flustered. You're going from playing an action in pursuit of an objective to, in the next moment, indicating or face acting. As soon as you realize that you have your daughter on the phone, you have to quickly develop a new set of actions and objectives. You want to reassure your daughter while not simultaneously killing the ardor of your girlfriend who is still on the couch. The obstacle is your own guilt.

INDICATING

★ You're indicating. What that means is that you are trying to show the audience how you feel. Indicating, sometimes referred to as "face acting" or "playing a result," is an acting error. Emotions are automatic value responses and you can't act them. When you try to act emotions, you wind up playing results. Indicating springs from distrust of the audience. The audience is really smart and you must trust it to follow the action on stage. The truth is that they don't miss a trick, including that you are indicating. They would not, of course, use the actual word "indicating," but they would use some equivalent, like maybe "fake" or "unconvincing."

★ You're not acting. You're acting like you're acting. Big difference.

★ You're supposed to be happy and laughing in this moment but in truth you feel like crap. You'll laugh anyway just so the audience will know that happiness goes in this slot. That would be an acting error. I can remember a famous sequence in the old *Honeymooners* TV show where Ralph Kramden was supposed to be the host of a cooking show. He had on his chef whites and all. But he had terrible performance anxiety. He would make this god awful tense grin and say "Ha ha," whenever he felt he was supposed to appear happy and relaxed. It was of course hilarious—precisely because most people will recognize in themselves the tendency to behave that way when under duress.

★ I have even seen actors (new ones admittedly) who cannot even walk across the stage without indicating. They find it impossible to walk from point A to point B without telegraphing to the audience, "See? This is me walking!" Sigh...

HOOKS ON MEISNER

The late Sanford Meisner fathered an immensely popular approach to acting training called the Meisner Technique. Part of its appeal is that it starts with the simplest of basics—listening and responding truthfully. "The foundation of acting," he explains early in his book, *Sanford Meisner on Acting* (Vintage, 1997), "is the reality of doing." You don't pretend to listen, you really listen; you don't pretend to do something, you really do it. To illustrate this principle, he invented the "repetition exercise" in which two actors face one another and repeat things back and forth. It is good stuff, and I applaud it.

As brilliant as Sanford Meisner was, however, I have a problem with the emphasis that he gives to certain aspects of acting over others. The Meisner Technique is invaluable at helping a new actor understand what it feels like to truthfully do something. But in my view it does not put nearly enough emphasis on the implied contract that exists between actor and audience. An actor can be as truthful as the day he was born and it will not have theatrical value. Emotions are not inherently theatrical. You need actions, objectives, and obstacles.

In his book the great teacher takes one of his students to task for being too "audience-conscious." In his criticism of the actor, he references Stanislavsky's concept of "public solitude." The problem is that Meisner does not sufficiently explain what Stanislavsky meant by public solitude. Stanislavsky never taught actors to be unaware of the audience. He was merely pointing out that an actor should not chase the audience. The concept of public solitude came from his study of yoga. It was about concentration and solitude, but he never taught that this kind of solitude should exclude the audience, as one might presume from reading Meisner.

Please do not misunderstand me. I am a great admirer of Sanford Meisner and generally agree with him. He had many amazingly correct insights about the art. But I think he did not address the actor's transaction with the audience much because his students in the 1950s and 1960s were mostly experienced New York stage actors in the first place. They already had a feel for the audience when they began.

I contend that actors are, at root, shamans. You put a circle in the dirt and call the tribe together. When they get there, you had better have something more to show them than how truthful and emotional you are. And you had better never exclude them from what you are doing on stage.

★ The cure for overacting is to simplify, simplify, simplify. You overact because you don't trust the audience. My advice is that you give them (us) more credit.

★ Did you ever hear of an actress named Eleanora Duse? She was a contemporary of another famous actress named Sarah Bernhardt back at the end of the 19th century. Bernhardt was the last of the "old school" actors. She struck poses when she acted. Like if she was horrified at something, she would strike a pose that might have depicted horror in an old oil painting. Eleanora Duse was a self-taught Italian actor who wanted to motivate each moment. She wanted to be emotionally truthful and came to fame because of it. In fact, Constantin Stanislavsky himself was hugely influenced by Duse. I am mentioning these women now because it is an acting error in the 21st century to act the way Sarah Bernhardt did. You do not want to strike poses or indicate emotion. The goal is to motivate and justify the moment. When Duse was embarrassed, she blushed!

★ I have noticed over time that you have developed an acting habit you need to break. Whenever a line might suggest emotional excitement, you adopt an emphatic tone. You tend to raise your voice and say whatever it is more clearly and more precisely.

That does not equate to being excited and, anyway, I think you are indicating, face acting. You're deciding what the emotion ought to be in that moment and then you're trying to come up with ways to act the emotion. It is the acting equivalent of one of those old paint-by-number kits. With acting, you always start with a blank canvas and no numbered bottles of paint.

MISTAKES

★ Everybody makes mistakes on stage sooner or later. You'll forget your lines or break a prop or something. Your scene partner will suddenly go into a panic and freeze up on you. Most actors who have been around a while can tell stories all day about awful/ funny things that happened on stage. The key to handling them is to realize that the audience saw what happened. If you dropped a bowl and broke it, they saw it. You can't pretend it didn't happen. Go ahead and start picking it up even though that wasn't in the original scene or rehearsal. If you forget your lines, start improvising. You can't stop the show after all.

DEALING WITH REALITY

★ During your monologue, there was a heck of a racket out in the alley because the city was picking up garbage bins. I purposely did not stop you because I wanted to see how you handled the noise. What you chose was to pretend it wasn't happening. I think it would have been stronger, once you realized that the noise was going to go on and on, if you had included the noise in your consciousness. We all deal with noises all day. At a certain point, it becomes odd that you seem not to know all that banging and clanging is going on.

JUST ACT NATURAL

I remember once in a very high-stakes acting class in New York, I was working on a scene from Neil Simon's *Barefoot in the Park,* in which I had to enter an apartment out of breath. I figured I would jog in place backstage to get myself really out of breath. When I entered, it was all very honest. The problem was that I was hyperventilating and was about to pass out. The class was packed with more than forty students, and the teacher was one of the most famous in the world. I was about to pass out in front of the bunch of them, and my scene partner didn't have a clue what was happening to me. And so I sat down on stage and put my head between my legs and continued the scene. Afterward, the teacher complimented me for a totally brilliant acting choice, and I smiled graciously. He never knew that if I had not done what I did, I would have passed out.

★ Deal with the reality of what happens on stage. I noticed that the actors in the scene before yours accidentally left a bowl of potato chips on the table. You entered what was now supposed to be your apartment, a whole new scene. Did you notice the bowl of chips? Did it occur to you to eat a chip? I noticed that once you sat down you pushed the bowl back, but I got the impression you pushed it back because you thought it was not your property, that it belonged to the other actors. I saw it as a bowl of chips on the table in your apartment. Actually, I think it would have added something to the scene if you had munched on a chip.

★ I was on stage in a summer stock production of *Star Spangled Girl* once when a nice-size bat started chasing insects in the stage lights. The thing kept coming within an inch of my head. Finally, I crawled under a table and ad-libbed this: "Norman, the landlady said we can't have pets!" The crowd loved it.

OPENING NIGHT

★ Opening nights of plays are their own special brand of torture, especially if all the media critics are out front. The best tonic for it is to keep a good sense of humor. The legend is that director Mike Nichols went backstage to comfort a very nervous female star on the Broadway opening night of *Plaza Suite*. She was in her dressing room in a total state. He calmly sat down, took her hands in his, gazed into her eyes and said, "Hey, don't worry, love. It all depends on tonight, that's all." That caused her to laugh, and the rest is history. *Plaza Suite* was one of the greatest hits of all time.

ACTING WHILE YOU'RE SICK

★ If you must act when you have a bad cold, you have two options. You can incorporate the cold into your characterization, in which case you would carry tissues in your pocket. Or you can take an antihistamine or decongestant and dry yourself up. The option you don't have is to go on stage and hope nobody notices.

SEXUAL SITUATIONS

★ It's okay for you to lust after your scene partner if the script calls for lust. In the first place, there is nothing in the scene that says you have to have actual sexual relations with her, so she is perfectly safe regardless of how much you lust. And in the second place, unless she feels that you are actually coming on, she won't feel threatened enough to respond, which is the requirement of the scene. Don't worry about offending her. She can take care of herself.

★ I had a student some years ago who was trying to get actually turned on during a seduction scene on stage. She was rubbing her legs together and stuff. Seriously! I diplomatically took her aside later and spoke to her privately about it, explaining that the audience does not want to see her actually, for real, turned on. It makes the audience nervous to see that kind of thing. Reality on stage is not real reality. It is pretend. There is an implied contract between the audience and actors in which everybody agrees to pretend together. Postscript: That same student never did get many roles and after a while gave up acting altogether. She is today selling herself as a great acting coach.

★ You're coming off as rather asexual on stage, Fred. There is close to zero sexual energy between you and your scene partner. I'm not looking at this and concluding that you are gay, just that the scene needs a shot of testosterone. I don't want to pry into this aspect of your private life, but it appears to me that you are blocking sexuality for one reason or another. Could be you are worried how it might appear if your scene partner figured you were really turned on by her. Could be you're worried that your wife would worry if she knew you were pretending to be sexually turned on by another woman. Whatever is the case, this scene is simply going to lie there like a dish rag until you allow yourself to get a little primal. Acting is an art. It is pretending. And it is okay to be sexual. Just don't be asking your scene partner out for a date.

EATING ON STAGE

★ Good grief! What do you have in that sandwich? You're going to choke during the scene! Take smaller bites.

★ Don't eat chocolate on stage. It will make you phlegmy.

★ If you are eating on stage, make sure there is water nearby on the set just in case you were to choke.

★ Remember that when you are acting on stage, you have a lot more adrenaline flowing through you. It is easy to choke on food.

ALCOHOL

★ Don't mime the wine. We could all see the bottle was empty. You poured some empty air and then began to sip contentedly. That's just weird.

★ When a playwright puts liquor in a scene, he is giving you a gift. Liquor lowers inhibitions and loosens the tongue. You can do and say things when you are drinking that you would not otherwise. This is why college students invented frat parties.

★ Never drink actual alcohol on stage. It will throw your timing off, even if you think it won't. Substitute something like grape juice or apple juice or water.

★ You're drinking whisky like it's apple juice. Whisky burns a little when you swallow. If it is a really excellent single-malt Highland scotch, it burns a *lot*.

★ By the time the scene opens, you have already been drinking for some time. Your timing and sense of humor and inhibitions will already be affected. During the scene, they become affected even more. You get drunker as time goes by.

★ Liquor does more than make you slur your words. It alters your perception of things. Here's some homework for you: Go to a party and drink ginger ale or mineral water only. Do not consume alcohol. Watch your friends as they drink more and more liquor. Use the situation as an acting class.

PLAYING DRUNK

★ To play drunk, try to act sober. It is the hallmark of an inexperienced actor that, when called upon to portray the extreme effects of alcohol, he will stumble around the stage and slur his speech. In life (Shakespeare advised that the actor hold the mirror up to nature, remember?), when we feel drunk we try to remain in control because we want to make a favorable impression on our friends. If you are at a party and have too much to drink, you try to act cool. It is unattractive to appear out of control. The step-by-step acting approach to any external substance, whether it be liquor or cocaine or sleeping pills, is first to identify what the physical manifestations of the substance would be. Alcohol will slow you down and disjoint your thinking; cocaine will speed you up. Once you know what the physical effect would be, you allow that to happen to yourself. Then you act against it. If your muscles are super relaxed and if your thoughts are becoming a bit loopy, then try not to let anybody else know what is happening. The exception to this would be a social situation in which everybody is trying to act drunk, like with a bunch of sailors on shore leave. Even if they aren't feeling very drunk, they will emphasize the appearance of inebriation.

★ Be careful when playing drunk that you do not appear too drunk to play your action. There is a fine line between being loosey-goosey and being sloppy drunk.

SMOKING ON STAGE

★ If you feel you absolutely must smoke, don't inhale. But don't smoke those herbal cigarettes because they stink up the theater auditorium something awful.

EYE CONTACT

★ In life, we make eye contact only about 20 percent of the time we're talking with another person. The rest of the time we are glancing away while framing new thoughts or processing what the other person is saying or scanning the horizon for predators. Eye contact is, in fact, a status negotiation. Try walking down the street making steady eye contact with people you pass. They will get annoyed with you, maybe even hostile. Occasionally you might get a date, but that's another matter. The fact is that we reserve steady eye contact for intimacy or for confrontation. I note that when you present your monologue, you fix your eyes on a single spot in the distance. It appears that you are making too-steady eye contact with the person you are talking to.

LYING

★ The eyes are the window to the soul. That's why a kid will avert her eyes when she is lying to you. On some level, she knows you will detect the lie if she looks at you directly. This same principle applies to your scene in *The Days of Wine and Roses.* You want your husband to take you back, but you are not willing to commit to sobriety. You are hiding your deep addiction from him. Yet if you were really hiding something from him, you wouldn't maintain such steady and unwavering direct eye contact, as I see you doing in this scene.

★ Your character is lying, but you don't have to signal to the audience that you are lying. I suspect that in life you are a much better liar than you are allowing your character to be.

CONVEYING NEED

★ As the scene begins, you're sitting in a restaurant, sipping wine and getting increasingly frustrated because, as you say in your opening line, "I want to have an affair!" Acting-wise, you need to get in touch with the needier side of yourself. You're saying the line now as if it is sort of an optional matter. No. This character doesn't just *want* to have an affair. She *needs* to have an affair.

★ Sarah, you have a line where you say, "I want to be married, you prick!" In your head imagine that you are saying "I need to be married, you prick!" Need carries a lot more acting voltage than want. I'm getting the impression that, if this thing with him breaks up, you'll be at a single's bar next Friday. No! This is the guy of your life! If this breaks up, you may very well become a nun!

KISSING

★ I understand that you don't want to kiss the actor you're working with. Maybe he doesn't want to kiss you either. Doesn't matter. The character you are playing is crazy about him and is a kissing fool. Don't impose your own values on your character. If you are going to play this character in my workshop, you're going to have to kiss the guy where and when it is called for in the script.

★ Uh...Joe, have you worked out that kiss with your scene partner? And are you sure your character would be planting such a suck-face open-mouth smacker on her in this current context? I mean, you are at her wedding, right?

★ I had a Muslim student in one of my acting classes a while back. He wouldn't do any scenes that involved kissing because it was against his religion. I let him slide with it but I told him he was going to have a dickens of a time as a professional actor if he would never kiss anybody. I've often wondered whatever became of that guy.

★ I know I've said this before, but if you're going to be involved in kissing on stage, don't eat any onions or garlic prior to the performance, and use breath freshener. Especially if you're a smoker, use breath freshener.

★ If you have a bad cold, you'll still have to do the kiss. Keep your mouth shut. No tongues. Wash your hands during intermission. Don't rub your eyes. Try not to give your cold to your scene partner. And, oh yeah, don't pick your nose.

BREAKUP SCENE

★ If you are playing a breakup scene or an argument, make the acting choice of being in love with the other character. It is harder and more theatrically interesting to break up with someone you love than with someone you don't like. And playing it this way holds a clearer mirror up to nature. When we break up with a lover, it is rarely because we have turned from love to hate. It is because we love the person but the situation is just not working out!

NEGOTIATING STATUS

★ We negotiate status all day long. Keith Johnstone wrote a lovely book about this idea, entitled *Impro* (Theatre Arts, 1989). Even space is a status transaction. If I get too close to you, I am invading your space. Though we may not negotiate out loud, you and I will negotiate about how close to you I can get.

ACTING WITH YOUR BODY

★ Don't act with your head. Your head is disconnected from your body. You need to act with your groin. Your life source is down there. This also goes for the girls.

★ You impress me as a passionate person, and yet when you act, the lower part of your body is almost totally disconnected from the upper part. Act with your whole self! It is okay to have sensations in your belly.

★ Growtowski had a marvelous idea. He would tell his student actors to pretend that they had a mouth on different parts of their body. I think you should try that because your energy is almost wholly above your shoulder line. Suppose your mouth was two inches below your navel? Suppose all of your energy had to come from there?

★ Use all of your senses when you act. Your scene takes place at a beach. Be aware that beach air smells fresh and salty.

★ See the room with more than your eyes. Be aware of the world around you with your entire body.

★ Listen to the other actor with your whole body, not just with your ears.

PORTRAYING ANXIETY

★ Blanche arrives at Stella and Stanley's New Orleans apartment already 70 percent toward a nervous breakdown. She's holding herself together with spit, chewing gum, and Old South pretensions. You need to find the source of this anxiety in your body before your first entrance. Remember that anxiety is a very heady energy. Most of Blanche's energy is above her chest line, and she is very light on her feet. She feels like she is about to float off the ground, and that her skin is too tight for her body. Imagine that a steel cable is pulling your spine erect, to the point where you are almost lifted off the floor.

NUDITY

★ I won't say that nudity is never appropriate, but I will say that whenever you take your clothes off on stage, it disturbs the theatrical transaction. Even in a play like *Equus,* when the character of Alan is justifiably naked while stabbing out the horses' eyes, the fact of his nudity is not lost on the audience. While he is involved in the passion of eyeball-stabbing, somebody out there in the audience is going to be considering the length of his unit. Nudity in film is a little easier for the audience to handle because the audience and the actor are not in the same room at the same time. I rarely see nudity on stage that is truly justified.

FURTHER THOUGHTS...

★ You know what? This scene feels constipated. What you guys need is an acting laxative. Let go! Allow the scene to surprise you! Stop controlling so much!

★ When you say one thing, you are deciding not to say other things. Every waking moment of your day is filled with choices. I am talking to you right now, but I could be home in bed.

★ Update that reference. Prostitutes don't cost $25 an hour any more. At least I don't think they do. Dave, what do prostitutes go for these days? Just kidding.

★ Don't make funny sound effects on stage. I couldn't believe it when you said "ring, ring!" and then answered the phone! It's sort of like pretending to scratch the cat's ears and then purring.

★ If you wear boxer underwear in a scene, wear a jock strap or some jockey style underwear underneath the boxers. Otherwise, your pecker might fall out. And if it doesn't fall out, you don't want to spend any time worrying that it might. Peckers tend to have a mind of their own anyway.

★ The playwright doesn't write in "oohs," "aaahs," sighs, and chuckles. He just writes the words. You add the sighs.

★ Why are you so physically static in the scene? You're supposed to be hosting a lunch for your good friend. Fuss over her a little! Pour her some fresh tea! Put out some cookies from time to time. Give her a foot rub or something. Ok, that may be going too far, but you get the idea!

★ Move! My God, you are rooted to the spot like an elm tree! It is perfectly okay to move on stage just as long as you have a destination or a reason.

★ Keep in mind when you are acting in *Waiting for Godot* that you are waiting for something. You know how you feel when you wait for a bus that won't come? And by the way, the word

Godot is pronounced "God-Oh," not "Ga-doh." They are waiting for God.

★ Find the humor in the scene, even if it is a knock-down drag-out fight.

★ Speaking a line is like tossing a ball. You have to make sure the other actor catches it.

Acting in Film

The best film actors enjoy displaying themselves in a very organic and truthful way in front of the camera. They are almost exhibitionistic in this regard. A camera makes some actors anxious the way a Peeping Tom would make them anxious if he peered into their bedroom. Such a person will tense up as soon as the director calls "Action!" and his performance will seem to be projected through cellophane. Other actors settle into a state of calm relaxation when the camera starts rolling. Actor Michael Caine says in his book *Acting in Film: An Actor's Take on Movie Making* (Applause Books, 2000) that the actor should deal with the camera as if it is a lover who will forgive him anything. Elia Kazan, in his autobiography, *A Life*, observes that film is more difficult than stage for an actor because the camera tends to look directly into your soul, like an X ray. It sees thoughts. On stage you can get away with temporary mental lapses but, if you lapse in front of the camera, it will see the glitch.

Acting itself is the same regardless of where you do it. It doesn't matter if you are on Broadway or on location with a movie in Katmandu, you still must play actions in pursuit of objectives, and you still must have theatrical intent. The distinctions between acting on film and acting on stage have to do with the medium, not the craft of acting itself. The most significant difference is that an actor on film does not have to physically deliver the performance to an audience via projection. The camera and microphone will do that for him. But here is where confusion begins for some aspiring actors. They erroneously come to believe that acting in movies is "smaller" acting. That conclusion could not be more wrong. Acting in film should still be of Shakespearean importance if it is to have theatrical currency. You adjust your performance for the medium of film and the realities of the editing process, but you do not act smaller.

When you act in movies and on TV, you rarely have the luxury of rehearsal. On a movie set, you get to run over the scene while they are setting up the camera and lights. Dustin Hoffman said in an interview that he considers film to be a more difficult medium than stage primarily because of the rehearsal deficit. He occasionally does not "find the character" until two or three weeks into shooting a movie. By then, it's too late to change anything because he has a chunk of scenes already filmed. It is rarely an option to go back and reshoot something just because the actor has a greater insight into the character and would play the scene differently if given the chance.

All theatrical productions are of course collaborations. Actors never work in a vacuum. There are directors, stage managers, writers, set designers, and costume designers, to name just a few, without whom you would not have a show. In film, however, there are a couple of extra and formidable collaborators: the cinematographer and the editor. At the end of the day, it is they, in consultation with the director, who decide how the final performances will appear on screen. They can make a mediocre performance seem stronger and an average-looking person appear to possess the beauty of Cleopatra. Film is a more overtly collaborative process for the actor because ultimately it all comes down to editing. Consequently, as an actor in a movie, you must always keep one eye fixed on what they will be getting in the editing room.

FIELD NOTES

STEPPING INTO THE SHOT

★ You have to step into this shot, Marc. Let me tell you how to do it. Put your foot on the mark on the floor. Then take three steps backward and stop. On "Action!" simply take three steps forward and you will be where you ought to be.

CROSSING TO YOUR MARK

★ There will literally be a mark on the floor, usually a small piece of gaffer's tape or something similar, showing you where to stop when crossing the room. Never look at your mark while you are crossing to it. The camera move will be timed to your cross. It drives the director crazy when an actor glances down at the floor to see his mark just prior to his cross. Most often they won't even save the take if you do that.

STANDARD COVERAGE

The standard movie scene is shot first with a *master shot,* which takes in the entire action of the scene; then they shoot *close-ups* of each actor. Sometimes they shoot a variety of close-ups—medium close, extreme close, and so on. If, however, they are shooting with a Steadicam (a shoulder-held camera), the camera is constantly moving. In that case, they don't usually have separate setups for close-ups.

CONTINUITY

★ Be careful about how you drink that glass of orange juice during the shot. Remember that the level of liquid in the glass has to be the same at the same moment in the master shot and then again when we shoot close-ups. Either take small sips or drink all of the liquid in one single point so the glass can be refilled to the same point each take.

CRASH COURSE IN CONTINUITY

Be very careful about how you handle props in a scene that you know will have standard coverage—master shots plus close-ups. You will have to handle the prop in the same way for each take. You can't pick up the glass of tea with your left hand in one take and with your right hand in the next take.

I remember when I learned this lesson the hard way. I was shooting a TV movie in which I was portraying a job counselor at an employment agency. I started fiddling with my pencil during the master shot. I would pick it up rather absentmindedly as I played the scene with an actress across the desk from me. It was actually a good reflection of what I do in life, and I still think it was an interesting acting choice. But, omigod, did it ever cause me grief! When we started shooting coverage, the script girl appeared at my side, reading from the notes she had made during the master shot. "When you said this line, you had the pencil in your right hand. When you said that line you shifted the pencil to your other hand." Suddenly what I had been doing absentmindedly had to be duplicated in close-ups. I had to use part of my brain to remember to shift the pencil here or there as I had done originally, and I think my ultimate edited performance suffered. The camera could see me thinking about the damned pencil. That was the first and last time I ever fiddled with a pencil while acting in film.

★ If you are working on a scene that will be shot with a master shot plus close-ups, be careful about talking at the same time you are physically moving from one place to another. In this scene, for instance, you have a marvelous exit line, but you are delivering it as you are moving toward the door. The editor will not be able to cut into that. Try walking to the door, stopping and turning back toward Jim, and *then* delivering that line.

CLOSE-UPS

★ In a filmed close-up, a raised eyebrow is an event. You can't bobble your head around like that!

★ During the last take, you continually slapped your thigh in order to emphasize points in the dialogue. Don't do that. In the first place, we are close up on your face and can't see your thighs, so we don't know what that slapping noise is and, in the second place, you shouldn't make a lot of superfluous movement when you are shooting film.

★ If we are shooting your close-ups across Paula's left shoulder, then we must shoot her close-ups across your right shoulder. If we do not do that, the eye-line of the actors won't work in the editing room. When they try to edit together the close-ups, co-ordinating with the master shots, the actors will not appear to be looking at one another. One will be looking slightly to the left and the other slightly to the right. Shooting the close-ups over opposing shoulders corrects this perception.

★ In a long shot, you can be as physically animated as you might be on stage in a theater. If, for example, the camera was positioned on one side of the street and your scene was being played on the opposing sidewalk, you would play it full-tilt. After the master shot, the camera will start coming in closer. The closer the camera, the more still you must be. In an extreme close-up, if you even nod your head up and down, it can be visually disorienting for the people in the audience.

★ If you want to appear more authoritative on camera, keep your chin down while your eyes glance upward. Harrison Ford does that kind of thing all the time.

★ The important part of moviemaking is in the close-ups. Many actors think of master shots as a kind of rehearsal, and they get serious about things only when the camera comes in close.

★ Jason, this is your close-up. It's okay for you to favor the camera. In reality, you might turn your head to the left on the pillow to talk to Martha but, if you do that, we can see only the right side of your face. I mean, it's okay to do that, but don't do it all the time. Split the difference. The editor will have better choices in editing if you do.

★ When you're shooting close-ups, try not to overlap the other actor's lines. Sometimes it is impossible to avoid, like when you are in the heat of an argument but, in general, you want to avoid overlapping. That way the editor can cut into the shots more easily.

★ With every glance you make, I sense that you really do not personally care for your scene partner. Get over it. You don't have to marry the man, but you do have to act with him. The camera can see thoughts. If you are thinking, "This guy is a creep," that is what the camera will see. And in this case, you're supposed to be loving him, not trying to get away from him.

> In the biz, film is generally thought of as a "director's medium" and stage as an "actor's medium" because, on film, the actor's performance is cut up and re-assembled in the editing room and, on stage, the actor is 100 percent in control of her performance.

FITTING INTO THE FRAME OF THE SHOT

★ Hold that magazine a little higher in this medium close-up. I realize that in reality you'd go cross-eyed trying to read it at that angle, but it looks good on camera. You need to get the magazine in the frame of the shot. If you hold it where you could actually read it, we could not see the magazine on screen.

★ In life, we each have our personal space. Only intimates and family members are invited into your personal space, right? Well, when you are shooting a scene between, say, you and a florist selling you flowers, the two of you have to stand very close to one another for the camera. If you don't stand close, the camera itself will give the illusion that you are standing wa-a-a-ay far apart. You stand much closer than you would in a real-life situation, and this takes some getting used to. It feels unnatural to have a stranger in your personal space and it can cause you to involuntarily recoil. If you do that, the camera will see it. Try thinking of every scene partner in a film as family. Maybe that will help.

> A film shot is a construction. The director may have you standing on an apple box, twisted right or left, holding your shoulder so that it doesn't block the camera and so on. Shooting, especially in tight places, can be an engineering feat as much as an acting one.

SOUND

★ When you shoot a scene in a crowded and noisy room, like for instance in a restaurant or nightclub or school cafeteria, the background extras will be instructed not to make any noise. They do this so that your dialogue can be picked up on a clean soundtrack. If there is background noise, the editor can't cut into it. She would not be able to match the ambient background noise on a take-by-take basis. This leads to what can be the strangest acting experience in the world the first time you do it. There you are sitting at a table, talking as if the room has hundreds of noisy people in it. You pitch your voice so that your scene partner can hear you over the crowd noise. And all around you are these ghostly animated people laughing and dancing and drinking with no sound coming out of their mouths and with no music to dance to. It is a Felliniesque out-of-body experience. But you'll get used to it.

MIT OUT SOUND

The abbreviation MOS stands for "mit out sound." They use it when they are filming picture but are not recording sound. MOS is a very old industry term in fact, going all the way back to the days of early German film directors who could not speak English without an accent. Instead of saying, "We will shoot this without sound," Eric Von Stroheim would say, "Ve shoot dis mit out sound." I know this story sounds unlikely, but it is true.

★ If there are distracting background noises like fire engines, they won't be able to use the shot because it will not match in the editing room. If they want to use the shot anyway, the only other option would be to go into a recording studio and have you loop the sound. When you do that, you watch your own image on a screen and then re-record your dialogue. I once had to do almost an entire performance like that on a Warner Brothers western. The back lot of Warners is very near the Burbank airport, so we had airplane engines droning in the background. Clearly this would not work for a movie set in 1869.

★ You do not need to project your voice so much, Jeff, even though Sarah is on the other side of the room. The microphone is, what, two feet away from your mouth? You only need to project as if she were two feet away.

TRACKING SHOTS

★ A tracking, or dolly, shot is one in which the camera moves alongside the actors. It may be traveling on a metal track on the ground, like a locomotive, or it may be on a wagon with wheels. However they do it in a particular shot, the terms remain the same. Typically, this is the kind of shot used when actors have to, say, stroll on the sidewalk while talking to one another. The camera will track with them.

STEADICAM

★ Steadicam shots do not usually have coverage. It is a one-take deal, and the takes tend to be long ones. They frequently involve a lot of movement on the part of the actors, like if they must talk while walking up or down a stairwell. The Steadicam operator simply walks along with them as they walk and talk. I participated once in a Steadicam shot that was twelve minutes long, an eternity on film.

STARTING AND STOPPING

★ Wait until you hear me say, "Action!" Joy. You keep jumping in too soon, starting the scene when I say "Rolling..." Wait for "Action." Even after that wait a short beat.

★ Keep the action going until you hear the director say, "Cut." Even if you make a mistake, don't stop the scene until the director says to.

HAPPY ACCIDENTS

In the movie *On the Waterfront,* take a particular look at the playground scene, in which Eva Marie Saint and Marlon Brando are walking across the asphalt and talking. During filming Saint accidentally dropped one of her gloves and Brando scooped it up and put it on his own hand! The director, Elia Kazan, kept the camera rolling. Now that I've told you this, you will see Eva Marie Saint trying to figure out what to do about the glove. But it was an accident at the time. Sometimes the best moments on film come from accidents like this. That is another reason to keep the action going even if you think you have screwed up.

REACTIONS

★ Yes, film acting depends a lot on reaction shots. Acting is reacting, and they tend to cut to reaction shots in the editing room. But it is still true that you, as an actor, must be playing an action in pursuit of an objective while overcoming an obstacle. Just because you are acting in front of a camera doesn't mean the rules of acting go out the window.

★ Listen. React. Speak. Listen. React. Speak. The camera wants to see you reacting. You must learn to allow reactions when shooting. You don't want to act the reaction because that is bad acting. You can't play results, remember? What you're doing is indicating your reactions. This is another reason why tension is Enemy Number One for an actor in a film. Tension blocks you and renders organic reaction impossible.

> I think it was Yul Brynner who used to say that the secret to acting in films is to think fast and talk slow. I like that.

★ Don't rush your reactions. You need to slow down your body clock just a bit when you are filming close-ups. Watch an actor like Kevin Costner. His filmed reactions typically are slow. But if you watch him work in his very earliest movies, like *Testament*, you'll see that the slower reaction time is something he acquired with experience. The camera likes to see you thinking and reacting. If your reactions are too long, the editor can simply cut around them in editing.

BLUE SCREEN

There is something known as *blue screen* acting. This is when you have to act with an animated creature or perhaps have to see something that isn't really there. They will have you act in front of a huge blue screen. Then, in editing, they will layer in whatever they want you to be interacting with. I recall once playing a fireman. I had to run up a ladder in a parking lot of 20th Century Fox on a sunny afternoon, with the blue Los Angeles sky in the background. When I saw the final scene on TV, they had put a burning building in there!

THE CINEMATOGRAPHER

★ Make it your business to get acquainted with the cinematographer on the set. Technically, he is not supposed to direct you and will always defer to the director. However, the cinematographer can tell you if you need to adjust your body this way or that in order to come across better on camera. I have long made it a practice after most takes to cast an inquiring glance at the cinematographer: "Thumbs up? We okay?" If he doesn't like what you're doing, he'll usually give you an unobtrusive signal about how to adjust. It can be very helpful for the actor to foster this kind of relationship.

> When you are auditioning or acting on camera,
> the director may refer to *camera right* or *camera left*,
> which is from the camera operator's perspective.
> In other words, camera right and camera left is, to the actor,
> backward of stage right and stage left in the theater.

ROLE MODELS

★ Al Pacino gave a veritable master class in film acting in a so-so movie entitled *Insomnia*. It's available for rental. Check it out. I also very much like the film work of Juliette Binoche. Take a look at *Blue* and *The English Patient*. *Tender Mercies* and *The Great Santini* are worth watching back to back for Robert Duvall's performances. He's an actor's actor in the first place and is brilliant in front of the camera.

Career Strategies

The only constant in the pursuit of an acting career is that it requires grit. There is no single "right" way to become an actor, and all the rules are made to be broken. This much is true though: If you want to be a professional actor, particularly in the United States, you will have to compartmentalize your brain to serve two masters—art and marketing. Acting is a reputedly glamorous career field in which there are many more applicants than there are jobs. This state of affairs tends to drive salaries down and make hardball career strategies a necessity. Further, there is not a direct correlation between talent and reward in acting. I have known many sensitive and insightful artists who lack the stomach and fortitude to organize the financial end of an acting career. They love to act but they hate the pursuit of talent agents and casting directors. The first time they come face to face with the kind of rejection that is routine during the pursuit of an acting career, they withdraw from the field and content themselves with acting for free in community theater.

The decision to become a professional actor is an emotional one, the same as it is with any art. Acting is, after all, an art like music, painting, and sculpture. Deciding to be an artist is like deciding to become a priest or rabbi. You don't say to yourself, "Well, I think I might like to be either an architect, a brain surgeon, or an actor."

You wake up one morning and realize that this is something that you simply must do regardless of the hassles. Most people enter the profession without a lot of support from their families. Parents are justifiably concerned about their children's financial well-being, and one does not enter any of the arts because of the prospects of financial reward. It is worth remembering that Van Gogh sold only one painting in his lifetime. Eighty-five percent of union-member actors in America earn less than $5,000 per year from their craft. In the U.S., we tend to equate art with commerce and so the government does not lend much support. The city of Paris, France, alone spends more on the arts in a single year than does the entire U.S. government. What this means is that if you want to be a professional actor, you are on your own. You will have to figure out how to make a living from doing it. This requires clear-headed career strategies, a good sense of humor, and a lot of discipline.

The money—but not a lot of the art—is in television, which is, after all, primarily a sales medium. If you are planning a long acting career, it is wise for you to exclude no opportunities. Unless you are a movie or television star, your career will be a crazy-quilt mix of stage, film, and TV. Commercials pay more money to union-member actors than movies and TV shows combined. Stage pays almost nothing, even on Broadway. You would be hard pressed to marry and raise a family while being dependent solely on income you might derive from stage acting.

I urge my students to consider what are their true motivations for coming into acting in the first place. Too many people who aspire to an acting career do so for the wrong reasons, and they are setting themselves up for a fall. They are motivated by a desire to be stars more than they are to be artists. As they will come to discover in time, there isn't anything you can do to become a star. It is an illusive pursuit, dependent more on timing and pure old fool's luck than it is on talent and tenacity.

Some people will tell me right off that they have no interest in stage at all. "I just want to act in movies and on TV," they explain. This is a red flag. Why would a person aspire to act only in movies and TV? What could a new actor possibly have against the legitimate theater? The very roots of acting are in the theater because that is the only place where actors and audience get together at the same time for a common purpose. The further away from the stage you move, the more distance you put between the audience and actors via cameras and movie or TV screens, the more strained becomes the implied theatrical contract between performer and audience.

Please do not misunderstand me. I am not implying that the stage has greater value than film. Artists will ultimately find a way to express themselves regardless of the medium—even in television. What I am questioning are the motivations for coming into acting in the first place. Many young people have grown up on a diet of TV and movies alone, and some of them may never have set foot in a theater. I react with a double take when a new student admits that he has never acted in a play and yet aspires to an acting career. On the other hand, I think it is going to be difficult for someone who aspires to act only on stage. The point I am trying to make here is that the design of a successful acting career involves balance.

TRAINING

If my own daughter wanted to be an actor, I would wish for her a four-year college education in a good liberal arts college that has a drop-dead wonderful drama department. Schools like Northwestern, New York University, UCLA, and DePaul fit the bill. After undergraduate work, I would encourage her to get an MFA from one of the more selective colleges, like Yale for instance. If she wanted to go the conservatory route instead of the university route, I would hope she could get accepted by an institution like the Juilliard School in New York.

The reason for this is because, in the entertainment industry, there is a pecking order to things. There are talent agents and casting directors who traffic mainly in the selling of actors for leading roles, and there are talent agents and casting directors who traffic mainly in small roles like waiters and cops and desk clerks. If you graduate from any of the very selective high-caliber programs I mentioned in that last paragraph, you will almost automatically catch the eye of the upper-echelon talent brokers, and your career stands a better chance of being jump-started. This is a preferable career strategy than to simply enroll in an acting class somewhere and to start chasing roles.

This is, as I say, the advice I give a young person. But there is no "right" time to become an actor or artist of any stripe. You do it when you must. Many people do not begin the pursuit of acting until they are in their late twenties or older. For them, the prospect of spending years in university programs doesn't make a lot of sense because of the age factor. In their case, it is arguably the best strategy to just get on with it. They should find the best professional-level acting training they can, have some photographs taken, and start going to auditions.

My good friend and former Los Angeles student Janet Rotblatt did not seriously pursue acting until she was in her fifties. She subsequently enjoyed a very successful thirty-year career, working steadily in Hollywood movies and TV shows as well as acting in a lot of stage productions. And she is not the first person I have seen achieve success after starting late.

FIELD NOTES

THEATRICAL PUBLICATIONS

★ The largest theatrical publications in the U.S. are *Daily Variety, Hollywood Reporter,* and *Back Stage* newspapers (*Back Stage* is in New York, *Back Stage West* is in Hollywood). *Variety* and *Hollywood Reporter* are mainly oriented to the production end of the entertainment industry. I personally subscribe to *Daily Variety* because it provides me with an overview of the industry and lets me look at what might be coming next year. Neither *Variety* nor *Hollywood Reporter* have casting notices for actors. *Back Stage* is the actor-friendly publication and contains a lot of casting notices. Just keep in mind that while *Back Stage* is a very good source of casting information for low-budget, no-budget student, and indie films and stage plays, if money is on the table for an acting job, casting directors will almost always contact talent agents to find actors.

PERFORMING UNIONS

★ If you are a going to be a professional actor, you will sooner or later have to join one or more of the performing unions. They are Screen Actors Guild (SAG), the American Federation of Television and Radio Artists (AFTRA) and Actors' Equity Association (AEA). Most acting jobs that pay money are union jobs. What that means is that the producers have signed agreements with the appropriate unions, thereby gaining access to union-member actors. I am, for example, in SAG. That means I cannot work in a non-SAG production at all. If I do so, SAG will fine me and, if I do it repeatedly, I could be kicked out of the union.

★ You cannot just go downtown and join the unions. Even if you could, I wouldn't recommend it because once you are in the unions, you can't do non-union work. Non-union work is good for building your experience and your resume. My advice is that you not join any of the performing unions until you must.

TRAINING

★ When you are looking for an acting teacher, try to audit a class before you start writing checks. The wonderful thing about auditing is that acting classes are unpredictable, and you get to watch the teacher in a dynamic situation. You might sit in on a class in which there is a melt down, and it would be highly instructive to see how the instructor deals with such things. A good mix is electric, but safe.

★ In general, you should be skeptical of acting schools that advertise in the mainstream press. The best professional-level teachers and schools don't advertise much outside of the trade press. *American Theatre* magazine and the *Back Stage* newspapers are good resources, for example. But if you hear a radio commercial for a modeling school, that's probably a no-no.

★ In addition to scene study, consider taking classes in clowning, improvisation, and dance. Singing lessons are swell, too.

★ Acting class isn't the only place to get training. The best acting training of all is to simply get into stage plays. The more you get up in front of audiences, the better it will be for you.

PHOTOS

★ Your headshot is your most important sales tool and you should give it the proper attention. It is well worth the money to pay a really good theatrical photographer, even if you have talented friends who will shoot some film of you for free. Theatrical photographers generally are familiar with the local market. They know what the talent agents are looking for in terms of photographs. They know what sells. The best way to find a good photographer is through references. Look at photos of other actors. Ask who took them. Talk to other actors in acting class. The least trustworthy guide to good photographers is paid advertising in newspapers. Though the best photographers in a given market may run ads in theatrical publications, you can also find a lot of turkeys there.

★ If you don't currently have many actor friends, you can always telephone local union-approved talent agents and ask them which photographers they recommend. You can get a list of these agents from the Screen Actors Guild Web site, www.sag.org.

★ Most actors have two headshots, one for commercials/comedy and another for theatrical/drama. If you are the type of actor who is likely to be cast in comedy roles mostly, you can probably get by with a single upbeat shot. A good commercial photo should emphasize your winning sense of life and good nature. They like happy campers in commercials. A good theatrical shot can also emphasize your good nature, but you can tilt a little more toward the artist in you. In other words, your theatrical shot can be a bit more cerebral, and your commercial shot can be a little more physical. And by the way, you don't have to always wear black in a theatrical shot.

★ Your headshot is maybe too sexy, love. Too much cleavage. When I look at the picture, my eye is drawn to your chest instead of your face. Not good. This shot is going to get you dates instead of acting jobs.

★ I like a three-quarter-length headshot at times because it allows people to see more of your body. A three-quarter-length shot is the type you might get if you were photographed sitting on a stool. It would capture your head to maybe hips or upper legs.

★ Your standard 8 x 10 headshots should be black-and-white. Only models use color shots for standard handouts.

★ Color shots are good if you are sending the images across the Internet. When you get headshots taken next time, ask the photographer to take one roll of color film.

★ I don't like the lighting in this shot, Larry. It's a good picture of you, but the photographer didn't give you the right light for your skin tone. African-American skin sometimes needs a different light or will tend to lose texture in the photo reproductions.

★ Osvaldo, this headshot makes you look a lot like a young Tom Cruise, which I suppose is swell, but that is not how you look walking around town. In the first place, you have worn glasses every time I have seen you in class. That suggests to me that you will wear them when you go to auditions or meet agents. I suggest you therefore wear them in your photo. Either that or invest in contact lenses. Also, your hair in this photo is a lot shorter than your hair now. They'll cut you a little slack on this, but it really is best to have a headshot that looks exactly like you.

★ When you get an acting gig in a movie, TV show, or commercial, take a 35mm camera with you. Once you are in costume and everybody has settled into the routine of work, maybe you can get one of the crew to snap a couple of pictures of you. There are frequently very excellent photographers around movie sets. Now, don't get yourself into trouble! Some directors don't like it if you start shooting pictures on the movie set. So take a camera, but maybe you should have the actual photos taken off to the side or something. I don't want you to get fired while following my advice.

★ Photo postcards are worth their weight in gold. These are not the kind of postcards you send to Aunt Minnie telling her the weather is nice in Bermuda and you wish she was there. These are theatrical tools, same as your headshot. Use them to stay in touch with agents, casting directors, and anybody else you may have met. I recommend that you order them in the 4- by 6-inch dimension because those will also fit inside a #10 letter-sized envelope. There may come a time when you want to drop a note to a person and you would like to enclose a photo postcard so that the recipient knows what you look like.

RESUME

★ An actor's resume is not like the kind of resume you submit if you are seeking a job at General Electric. A theatrical resume is all about your acting background. You could hold a master's degree in psychology or be a licensed architect and it wouldn't matter as much on the resume as an acting credit.

★ On a resume, you don't want to write stuff like "long range goals" or "strengths and weaknesses." I've seen new actors do that kind of thing and it almost always falls flat, even when done with humor. It just broadcasts that you're a beginner.

★ I don't think it is a good idea for women to write their home addresses on their resumes. You just never know where these photos might wind up. Some idiot might pull one out of a garbage can somewhere, and you wouldn't want him to know where you live. It is okay to put your contact info in a cover letter, and it is fine to list a voice-mail or cell phone number on the resume itself.

★ The more credits and experience you acquire, the less personal information you should include on your resume. At the far end of the spectrum, a star like Julia Roberts probably doesn't use a resume at all. At the near end of the spectrum, a beginner may have only high school acting credits to list. I remember when I started out I had my hair color, height, weight, acting teachers, all sorts of things listed on the resume. After I had appeared in a hundred TV shows, my resume had my name and agent's logo at the top, followed by a list of shows and billings.

★ It's okay to print your resume directly on the back of your photo, but I recommend you run off only a few at a time. That way you can update your resume without getting more photos made.

★ If you want to give the illusion of recent acting activity, omit a credit or two when you prepare your resume. Then write them in longhand prior to going to an audition.

★ Do not put work as an extra on your resume. Extra work is not considered acting. Extras provide a background against which the principal players perform. I realize you want to flesh out your resume, but that's not the way to do it. And whatever you do, never lie about the degree of your work in a feature film or TV show. If you were an extra, then leave it off the resume. Don't write something on your resume that vaguely suggests you had lines. Lies of that sort may very well come back to haunt you one day.

★ If you don't have enough credits to fill out a resume, then just summarize your background in a cover letter that accompanies your headshot.

TALENT AGENTS

★ If your talent agent is not sending you out on enough auditions, try going into the office and asking what you can do to jumpstart things. Do *not* go in there and blame them for not sending you out. That will make them defensive and will likely get you nowhere.

★ If you want to change talent agencies, don't drop agent number one before you are successfully signed to agent number two. And, yes, it is okay when pursuing new representation to have your current agent's contact info on the photo. Simply add your own home number and address at the top of the resume. Trust me on this, agent number two is not going to call agent number one to ask about you or why you might be seeking new representation.

> If an acting job pays money, there is almost certainly going to be a talent agent and casting person in the middle of the transaction.

★ When you are first signed by a talent agent, it is a good idea to maintain a visible profile for a while. Drop by the office now and then just to stick your head in and say hello. Don't make a pest of yourself, but once they have you on their client list, help them keep you in the front of their minds.

DIFFERENT KINDS OF AGENTS

You need to have two talent agents in Hollywood: one for "theatrical," which in that city is movies and TV shows, and one for commercials. You want to be very wary about signing with a single "full-service" agency in LA. Full-service agencies that handle both theatrical and commercials under one roof do exist in Hollywood, but they historically have not fared well. Full-service agencies are financially successful in New York, and are the norm in every other U.S. city I can think of. Hollywood is different. The reason for this is that, in the beginning, the talent agencies in Hollywood served the movie industry, which was always lucrative. When Madison Avenue came along in search of actors for commercials in the 1950s and 1960s, the movie agents weren't interested. And so a few entrepreneur agents decided to open agencies that served only the commercial market. In New York, the talent agents originally served only the legitimate theater, and theater has never been lucrative. So when Madison Avenue knocked on *their* doors, the agents figured they could use the extra money, and so they started running commercial representation out of the back room.

★ Beware of talent agencies that are attached to acting or modeling schools. And if a talent agent insists that you go to a particular school, that is a red flag. He may be getting kickbacks.

★ If you want to get an agent on the telephone, try calling early in the morning or late in the afternoon when the receptionist is likely not to be at work.

★ When you go to an interview with a talent agent, it is a good idea to have a contemporary monologue prepared in case you get the chance to present it. Usually, a comic monologue is the best choice because most agents make their money from light-hearted fare.

RESIDUALS

★ You make a living in acting because of residuals. After you shoot a commercial, they pay you for the session and then again every time it runs. When you make a TV show, same thing. Heck, I still get little checks for things I shot fifteen years ago! After about twenty reruns of a TV show, the checks decline to something like five dollars, but they still come in. With commercials, the residuals are paid on a declining scale that starts again at the top of every thirteen-week cycle.

WORKING WITH A BAD SCRIPT

★ I learned more about acting from doing bad plays off-off-Broadway than I ever did by acting in perfect plays by Tennessee Willliams or Arthur Miller. When you act in a famous play, you know going in that it works. A bad play may not work, but you still have to make it work. Or appear to be working. The audience will not look at you and cut you slack because the writing is bad. They'll think you're a bad actor if you don't make it work.

★ You had better get used to taking small roles and making them into something. When you get to Hollywood, you will be lucky if you are offered roles at all. And you will be triple-lucky if the roles you are offered have any substance. The greater likelihood is that you will be playing supporting roles for a while, second leads at most. You'll discover that these roles frequently are just an expositional device, something with which to advance story points. The burden will be on you to make them interesting.

★ Acting students usually learn their craft by working on famous plays. This is good because it teaches you what high-quality actually looks and plays like. But when you get into the real world, you'll find that not everybody is as idealistic as they were in acting school. And not all of the writing is swell. In fact, a lot of it is downright awful.

★ The head of casting at Columbia Pictures Television told me once that she loved to have me in on auditions because she knew I would make whatever I did interesting, even if the role was badly written. In Hollywood, the writer brings the words, and the actor brings the character.

ROLE MODELS

★ Study good actors and then try to copy what they do. I have learned a lot from watching the work of Al Pacino, for example. He is a master at working out internal but unspoken conflict. And I have studied the work of Charlie Chaplin to the point that I have worn out my DVDs. It is okay to steal ideas and techniques from excellent actors. Just make sure that what you are looking at is worth stealing.

★ Be careful which actors you choose to emulate. Make certain you are emulating actual actors for starters. Stand-up comedians like Jerry Seinfeld, Gary Shandling, and Bob Newhart may be starring in their own sitcoms, but that doesn't mean they are actors. Mainly they are just playing themselves.

CUTTING CLASS

★ If you're considering cutting acting class one night, ask yourself if you are sick enough to cut a performance. Are you so sick that you would tell the stage manager to bring on the understudy? If not, then go to class. Acting requires that kind of commitment.

SELLING EYEBALLS

Television is a sales medium, not an art medium. From the beginning of broadcast television, the point of TV shows has been to attract the greatest number of happy, ready-to-buy consumers to the commercials. Behind the scenes in the biz, they call it "selling eyeballs." This partly explains why television shows are frequently so shallow in comparison to stage or film in terms of acting and plot. The last thing the producers and network want to do is to upset viewers or to unduly agitate them. This is why you don't see more actors like Robert De Niro on TV shows. They have about them an air of danger and are somewhat unsettling to the viewer, which is not conducive to selling product. TV wants its stars and show plots to be non-threatening.

FINDING YOUR "TYPE"

★ It is a good thing to be typecast when you are starting your career. It is good if an agent looks at your headshot and says, "This is a housewife" or "This is a construction worker." So before you run out and get headshots taken, try to figure out where you fit type-wise. The way to do this is to watch the commercials that run on TV shows that are targeted to your demographic group. Working mothers, for example, flock to the early morning talk shows. Then, instead of watching the shows themselves, watch the commercials. Go to the bathroom during the show. The people you see on the commercials are your competition. Study them carefully. Note how they dress and how they present themselves. Then make sure your headshot shows that you are competitive with them.

COMMERCIALS

★ If you want to act in commercials, you will need to find a talent agent who works in that field. In order to capture his attention, you should first have a good commercial headshot taken. A commercial shot—as opposed to a theatrical shot—is one that emphasizes your good and happy nature. Actors who succeed in commercials usually display a likeable, nonthreatening, and energetic persona.

★ The way it works with union-covered commercial residuals is that you are paid for reuse based on the number of TV viewers in a particular city. A commercial that runs for thirteen weeks in New York City will pay more than a commercial that runs in Dallas for the same period.

★ When you have a commercial that is running in x-number of cities simultaneously, but not on network TV, that's called "wild spot use."

★ Before I became fond of yogurt, I auditioned for a yogurt commercial. They had me eating the stuff and grinning. I thought I was going to throw up, but I kept grinning because I wanted the money and I knew in my heart that this stuff wouldn't really kill me. Even though it felt like it might.

★ If you are a strict vegetarian and absolutely will not do commercials for, say, McDonald's or Burger King, let your talent agent know about this when you first sign up with him. In fact, if you have any limitations like that, let them know. I, for example, have never done a commercial in which I had to have my shirt off because I have a birthmark. And I am very picky about commercials I might do for political causes or candidates.

★ The money is in commercials. The U.S. of A. is pretty much defined as a place where people sell things to one another. TV commercials are the heartbeat of the beast.

INTERNET DATABASES

★ Some entrepreneurs are selling aspiring actors space in Internet databases. For a fee, you get to post your photo and resume on their Web site. They will tell you that casting directors and agents can browse the photos when looking for talent. That word "can" is the catch. They can but *will* they? Not likely. When a casting director is casting a Robin Williams movie, he doesn't first sit down and start browsing Internet databases. He calls talent agents. What you need is well-connected and enthusiastic representation.

CASTING DIRECTOR WORKSHOPS

★ Especially in the major cities, you will find workshops in which you are basically paying to meet casting directors and/or talent agents. They can be very appealing because it is so difficult to meet these people. However, you should know that the workshops themselves are a sizeable cottage industry. Probably ninety percent of the time, actors who pay to meet casting directors are just tossing away their money. It doesn't lead to anything because when the casting director is casting a role on a TV show or a movie, she will call talent agents to find actors. Usually the casting director workshops are justified as "education," but that is like saying street people go to soup kitchens for the prayers. The primary transaction at casting director workshops is paying for access.

★ You should not have to pay to meet a casting director. Ever.

MODELING CONVENTIONS

★ I'm not a fan of these big modeling conventions you see advertised on TV and in the newspaper. They are dangling the prospect of stardom and using the presence of casting directors and talent agents as a carrot to get wannabes to write checks. It is the paid-access paradigm once again, and I do not think actors should be paying for access. There are no shortcuts in the acting business, and if you spend your money on modeling conventions, there is an overwhelming likelihood that you are just wasting it.

HOLLYWOOD

★ You can go to Hollywood whenever you want to, but my advice is that you get some training and build a resume first. Hollywood can be a daunting and merciless place despite all that sunshine and palm trees. A good plan would be to get some film of yourself before arriving in Hollywood. Do some student films and get copies of them. Hollywood agents like to look at film.

NEW YORK

★ New York is a great city. I lived there for the first nine years I was an actor and will always have a soft spot in my heart for it. It also is damnably expensive to live in New York, so be prepared for that. But do you know the song, "New York, New York"? It has a line in it that goes, "If I can make it there, I'll make it anywhere!" I suspect that is true. If you can become a working actor in New York, you will have earned your spurs.

CHICAGO

★ Chicago has over two hundred theaters in it and enjoys incredible community support. It is home to famous improv troupes and schools, theater companies such as the Steppenwolf Theater and the Goodman. Chicago is today sort of what off-Broadway in New York used to be twenty years ago: a hotbed of development for new plays. If you are new to acting, a move to Chicago might be a very good idea. Yes, winters there are cold. So what? Don't make career choices based on weather.

GETTING ALONG WITH OTHERS

★ Actors are some of the finest humans you will ever meet. They can also be screwy, self-involved, neurotic to a fault, and pushy. When plays and movies are produced, the cast becomes a kind of family for a while. Sometimes there is even romance, but I don't personally think that is wise. The key to getting along with everybody is to remember that you are in a professional environment. Maintain a strong sense of personal boundaries. Be professional yourself, making sure to show up for rehearsals and performances punctually. Know your lines when it is time to know them. Remember that the chain of command on the production starts with the director. Don't engage in destructive behind-the-scenes gossip or back-biting. A lighthearted production is a good production. Sometimes there will be personality conflicts. When that happens, try not to add fuel to the fire. The important thing is the show. Don't allow yourself to be seduced into "taking sides" in cast conflicts. Keep your eye on the ball. What you want is a successful production. Anyway, you'll find that most actors work with the same directors and actors again and again. It makes sense to be known for your professionalism and good nature.

COMMUNITY THEATER

★ You have a considerable amount of experience in community theater, Barbara. I think you have come to a point where you need to make some decisions about whether you want to be paid to act or not. If you decide you do want to be paid, then you should raise the standard of your acting. Community theater is fun, but its problem for the aspiring professional actor is that the audiences are very forgiving. They realize that nobody is getting paid, so the whole affair has a Mickey Rooney "Hey, guys, let's put on a play!" quality. There really is a difference between the acting quality you see in most professional theaters and that of most community theaters.

★ I have known people who were literally stars of the community theater circuit, going from one show to another, but they never made it on Broadway or in a movie. You need to decide if you want to be a big fish in a bathtub or a little fish in a big sea.

CASTING CALLS

★ Type-wise, it is better to be on the younger end of an older call. In other words, if you are going to fudge your look one way or the other, go older, not younger. Even if you can successfully make yourself pass for twenty-two instead of thirty in a certain light, you are asking for trouble by doing so. The agents may send you into auditions against actual twenty-two-year-old women, and they will get the parts. Anyway, you want to age into your call, not away from it. If you are on the younger end of an older call, you will get better the older you get.

EXTRA WORK

Working as an extra in most movies is not really acting. Acting is an interpretative art. Extra work is a non-skill. Any random sampling of people at a shopping mall can do extra work just fine. If you really want to have a career as an actor, I advise you not to do a lot of extra work on movies. Do it once or twice just for the curiosity value, but don't kid yourself into thinking that just because you are on the set with working actors that you are their artistic equal. Extras help provide a background against which the principal players play. In general, they are not treated on set with anything near the same level of respect as the principal players.

The exception to this rule is in commercials. It is increasingly common for producers to hire talent as extras and then decide who is a principal player once they get the footage into the editing room. It is a matter of economics, not art. Extras cost less than principal players and, in commercials, there is not even any dialogue half the time. If you get upgraded from extra to principal in a commercial, it can mean many thousands of dollars more for you. If you get upgraded from extra to principal on a movie, which is wildly unlikely in the first place, it will not amount to very much monetarily.

APPEARANCE

★ Eytan, you and I both need to lose some weight around the middle. You are allowing all of your characters to sort of slouch because that has become a comfortable posture for you in life. Your body is your instrument. You need to keep it tuned up.

★ Even your best friend won't tell you, love, but your hair color and style are awful. It is too blonde and too permed. To be candid, it looks very small town, like you would see at a local mall. If you are going to play hardball in the entertainment industry and start demanding that you be paid to act, you need to upgrade your look. Spend the money on consultation with a top-notch hairstylist, preferably in a large city. Stay away from the local beauty parlor.

★ Notice that, in TV commercials, women over thirty tend to have shorter hair. As a general rule, longer hair goes with younger women. Shorter hair is easier to deal with.

★ Get your teeth fixed.

★ You probably should lose about twenty pounds. It's not fair, but women have more of a problem with weight perception in the entertainment industry than men. I'm not suggesting that you do anything unhealthy, but I think you'll get more work if you slim down.

★ How long have you had that beard? It is a limitation for acting in commercials. It won't hurt you as much theatrically, but in commercials they don't like facial hair unless you are playing a mountain man. I'd hate to see you have headshots taken with the beard and then have your agent ask you to go shave and do an expensive reshoot. Tell you what. How about if you schedule your headshot session and go with your beard intact. Let the photographer run off a roll of bearded shots. Then shave and do a couple more rolls clean-shaven? Then you'll have bearded photos you can show the agent or casting director so he can see what you would look like with the beard. That would be much better than having only a bearded shot and telling them that you are willing to shave if you get a role. Seriously, these folks will have a lot of trouble imagining what you will look like. If they don't see it in a photo, they'll think it doesn't exist.

★ You know, they have dental bonding now that is inexpensive and painless and will cosmetically correct that chipped tooth you have. I'd do it if I were you.

★ You have a poor body image, which will eventually hurt your acting. Listen, you don't have to have a perfect body in order to be an actor. Hardly anybody has a perfect body anyway. The important thing is that you own and be proud of the body you have, and that you be healthy.

DEALING WITH REJECTION

★ Rejection comes with the turf. Get used to that reality and do not take it personally.

> The good news for you is that most great artists go through the same sort of agonized soul-searching you are experiencing. Van Gogh ultimately cut his ear off over it. I wouldn't advise going that far though.

BREAKING THE RULES

★ There are no rules in the pursuit of an acting career. I once called a director who was on the Queen Elizabeth 2 boat in the middle of the ocean. I did so because I had read that he was headed for New York, and I wanted to audition for his movie. Yes, I got the audition, which was a big deal seeing as I didn't have an agent at the time.

SELLING YOURSELF

★ In general, you won't get into trouble by being inventive and aggressive in selling yourself as an actor. Read Dale Carnegie's old book *How to Win Friends and Influence People*. Even though it is about seventy years old, it contains excellent advice. Keep a smile on your face and offer a warm handshake and nobody is going to fault you for trying to sell yourself.

> Know how Michelangelo got his nose broken? When he was a kid, he boasted to another kid about how he was the better painter. The other kid popped him one. Greatness recognizes itself.

★ There is such a thing as being too pushy when trying to sell yourself. I knew a lawyer who was trying to break into acting, and he sent an agent a subpoena. Bad idea. The agent was horrified. I knew another actor who sent a female agent one silk stocking and told her she could have the other one if she interviewed him. Nope, not a good idea. On the other hand, I knew an actor who posed as a pizza delivery guy and delivered a pizza to a big casting director's office. Under the pizza was his plastic-wrapped photo and resume. He got an interview.

LEARN TO PLAY COMEDY

When I came into acting, I did not want to play comedy at all. I thought I had a Chekhovian heart and sensitivity to the darker corners of the human condition. I wanted to act in *Hamlet* and *Death of a Salesman,* and I wasn't much interested in anything but stage.

So what happened? I got out of acting school, did a season of summer stock to sort of get my feet wet, and started knocking on agents' doors in New York. Agent after agent told me I would be good for comedy. Nobody seemed to care how serious I was. In due time, I started getting auditions, first for commercials and then for comedic stage plays. When I got to play "serious" roles, it was because I had been hired for a season somewhere and they filled in my calendar with whatever was available in between comedies. On occasion, that meant I got to do serious drama.

The bottom line is that I soon realized that, if I wanted to make a living as an actor, I had better learn how to play comedy. It became clear to me that this was where the money was. It was, however, my good fortune to have come at the whole subject with a preference to do drama because I also quickly learned that comedy is drama plus. It is drama with a kick, drama with something extra. If you want to play comedy successfully, you first make the scene work as a drama. You do not set out to be funny.

MAKING ENDS MEET

★ Launching an acting career is like launching any other career. You need to arrange your financial affairs so that you can make a living while you are pursuing it. Actors traditionally have worked as waiters and bartenders and caterers because those sorts of jobs pay a high hourly wage and do not demand a lot of career commitment. Also, they allow you to have your days free to chase agents and go to auditions. It is almost impossible to pursue a professional acting career while you are working at the electric company full time.

★ You will hear it said that there are no small roles, only small actors. I heard that piece of idealism, too, early on in my New York career. It is true in an artistic sense, but it is absolutely incorrect in a marketing and long-range career sense. You will do better career-wise if you think of yourself as a lead performer.

SELLING YOURSELF IN HOLLYWOOD

In television shows, they put a high premium on a fast-study, one-take kind of actor. They will actually reward you for doing the kind of work that will get you into trouble in your acting class. I know that when I teach acting, I admonish the actors not to leap to performance. In television though, the production schedule is break-neck. You shoot a scene two or three times and move on. It's not like making a movie where they may do the same scene over and over again.

Also, because TV scripts are, on average, pretty awful, directors and producers like it if you are the kind of actor who can make a silk purse out of a sow's ear, theatrically speaking.

VOICE-OVERS

★ Voice-over work is wonderful. You don't even have to shave. But it's expensive to get started in it. You need to have a demo tape, and that can cost several hundred dollars to produce. I have known some people to spend upwards of $5,000 on classes and demo tapes and still not have an agent. Also, keep in mind that the voice-over market favors male voices. Madison Avenue believes that male voices sell better than female voices.

WORKING IN CARTOONS

★ Cartoon voices are largely recorded in Los Angeles. If your goal is to be a voice in animation, you may have to move there. You'll need a demo tape, same as you do with voice-overs for commercials. Being able to do multiple characters is desirable.

TURNING DOWN A ROLE

★ If you are offered a role that you think is awful, decline with grace. Say something to the director like, "I think this role is just not the right one for me, but I'm positive you're going to have a great success with it." Never burn bridges. Ours is an industry built upon relationships.

FAKING IT

The other day a very innocent aspiring teen actor asked me via e-mail if the producers of movies provide the actors with rubbers when they have sex in a scene. (I swear this is a true story!) Let me please make this very clear: You do not have to have actual for-real sex in a movie scene. When you go to a movie and see scenes in which it appears the actors are actually doing the wild thing, they are not. People only have real sex on film in pornographic movies, and you really do not want to be doing those. They are not good for your career.

REALITY SHOWS

★ If you want to try to get on one of the many reality-based television shows, by all means go for it. Just don't delude yourself into thinking that they have anything to do with acting. They have much more to do with achieving Andy Warhol's "fifteen minutes of fame."

HAVING OPINIONS

★ What do you think about things? Do you read the paper? Do you believe in God? Do you think the United States is God's chosen country? Do you believe in censorship? Do you believe in the military draft? Do you think it is okay to have sex on the second date? Actors are people with strong opinions. This is not to say that they are correct about anything, just that they have opinions, and that is what the audience wants to see. Heck, I think Shirley MacLaine is one taco short of a combo plate with all her talk about prior lives, but she still is a terrific actress. And I think a big reason she is so good is that she is willing to step out front and say what she thinks about things, even if those opinions are not popular.

★ The three words that every actor ought to totally expunge from his vocabulary are "I don't care."

> I don't think I have ever seen a really excellent actor who was not psychologically dysfunctional. Many actors come from god-awful childhoods.

MORAL OUTRAGE

Sometimes, I feel like I could teach a bear how to act. It isn't all that difficult for a person to learn how to stay in the moment, to listen, and to play an action. But acting technique alone will not make you an excellent actor. You have to have a bit of moral outrage. To be the kind of actor who gets the audience involved, you have to care about things. You have to care enough about things to fight for what you think is right. I'm not suggesting that you walk around looking for a fight or that you get out of bed angry every morning. You can be deeply benevolent and peaceful and still care about things. "Doesn't everybody care about things to some degree?" you may ask. Yes, of course everybody cares to some degree. But the true artist has a special responsibility. An artist must care and take a stand and be willing to fight for something. Moral outrage does not equate to a political position. It doesn't matter if you are left-wing, right-wing, capitalist, or communist. All that matters is that you care. Moral outrage can be expressed in whatever way you want to express it. And it can be transformed for use in a play or movie. If you are a hardcore right-winger, you can still portray a communist; if you are devoutly religious, you can still play an atheist.

RIGHT-TO-WORK LAWS

★ Some states have right-to-work laws. What that means is that employers are not bound to collective bargaining. If union actors go out on strike, the employer can simply hire non-union. These laws suck. Right-to-work laws are very anti-union, and actors really need their unions. Invariably, in states that have such laws in effect, union-member actors fare less well than in states where such laws do not exist.

CHARACTER ACTORS

★ Just because I said you are a character actor instead of a leading lady, that does not mean that you are not pretty. Most great actors are character actors. It's not an insult. You can still play leads. Anyway, a character actor is implicitly an actor who plays characters, right? Isn't that what you want to be? Heck, if I couldn't be a character actor, I wouldn't fool with acting at all.

CHARACTER VERSUS PERSONALITY ACTING

There are two kinds of actors in the world. There is the actor who wants to make every character fit his own street personality (TV shows are chock full of actors who work this way, especially if they come from the ranks of stand-up comedy), and there is the true character actor. Dustin Hoffman is a true character actor, as are Johnny Depp and Meryl Streep and Julianne Moore. Most of us, when we started acting in high school plays, dabbled with character acting. Even though we were too young for the roles, we played kings and queens and full-fledged adult characters. I think the best actors are character actors.

ENGLISH AS A SECOND LANGUAGE

★ If English is not your first language and you speak with an accent, your accent will be a casting limitation. It is a good idea to acquire a standard American accent that you can use when you need to. I hear non–American-born actors speak of the desirability of "accent reduction," but that is really not what happens when you change your accent. You will experience it as *acquiring* a new accent rather than losing one.

BAD REVIEWS

★ You are going to get bad reviews, take my word for it. My advice is that you not let it cause you to lose sleep. By the same token, don't let favorable reviews go to your head. A career is not based on a few reviews. Remain focused on the work.

BETA BLOCKERS

★ There are drugs on the market that will help you get over your nerves. Your doctor can prescribe them. I recommend that you be careful about going this route, however, unless your nerves are debilitating, causing you full-tilt panic attacks. Beta blockers can reduce your emotional reactions overall. Actors traffic in emotions. Ideally you will not drug yourself. I tried one of those beta blockers once and it just made me feel thuddy, sort of one step behind myself. I never tried them again.

GETTING FIRED

★ Actors get fired from time to time. It comes with the turf and you shouldn't let it ruin your life if it happens. I once lost an entire season of repertory because I came down with pneumonia. On another occasion, the director and I simply could not see eye to eye on the character I was playing. The thing to remember is that, when you must leave, do not burn bridges if you can help it. Though things may not have worked out well on this particular gig, there will be other days and other roles. My strong advice is that you develop relationships that last and can be trusted. It is okay if you must leave a cast, but it is more difficult to maintain those valuable relationships you've formed if you walk out the door cursing.

QUITTING

★ One of my many psychotherapists was a former Dominican monk. He quit the priesthood because he wanted to get married and wound up being a psychotherapist. I mention him now because I want you to know that it is okay to decide to quit acting. This is a terribly difficult profession in which to make a living, and it is full of stress. I love it, but I also know that a person must allow her context in life to evolve. If you come to a place where you are exhausted by the stress of pursuing an acting career, please do not feel bad about stepping back for a while. You can always return. It's not a big deal. There is no "right" time to become an actor and there is no "right" time to stop. The important thing is that you be happy in life.

Further Reading

I personally don't care much for recommended reading lists because they are usually too overwhelming. Also, I like to know more about a book than its title if I'm going to buy it. So what I'm doing here is a little more personal. All of the following titles are on my own bookshelf. There are easily twice this many more on my shelf that I read and value, but I want to make each entry comprehensive for you. I've thought hard about the following titles, asking myself which books would be essential reading and which would merely be highly recommended.

ESSENTIAL READING

Stanislavsky in Focus by Sharon M. Carnicke, Harwood/Routledge, 1998. Ms. Carnegie is Associate Dean of Theater at the University of Southern California. Her book is hands down the best I have ever read about the evolution of Stanislavsky's work and how it transferred to the United States. Indeed, I think this book is more useful to the new actor than reading Stanislavsky himself.

On the Technique of Acting by Michael Chekhov, HarperResource, 1991. Michael Chekhov was playwright Anton Chekhov's nephew and was an actor with Stanislavsky's Moscow Art Theater. He was considered a little loopy, if brilliant, in his day because of his religious ideas, but he later came to be highly respected. In particular, Michael Chekhov is responsible for introducing the concept of the "psychological gesture."

Sanford Meisner on Acting by Sanford Meisner, Vintage, 1987. Even though I do not personally endorse everything in this book, I consider it to be essential reading. The Meisner Technique is probably the most popular approach to acting training in the U.S., and new actors should be familiar with it.

True and False: Heresy and Common Sense for the Actor by David Mamet, Vintage, 1999. David Mamet is one of our major playwrights and he has some outspoken ideas about acting. I disagree with his objections to character analysis but agree with his general views on acting training. He's blunt and rough at times, but he makes a lot of good sense. New actors in search of training would be wise to read this one.

Audition by Michael Shurtleff, Bantam, 1979. This is the granddaddy of all the books about audition technique. I personally studied with Michael Shurtleff back in the 1970s and have been strongly influenced by his views.

Impro: Improvisation and the Theater by Keith Johnstone, Theatre Arts Books, 1989. Johnstone's approach to improvisation is marvelous stuff. His application of status transactions is good for improv as well as textual acting. I use Keith Johnstone's ideas frequently in my own workshops.

The Empty Space: A Book about the Theater—Deadly, Holy, Rough, Immediate by Peter Brook, Touchstone Books, 1995. I idolize Peter Brook. This man is one of the few you can safely categorize as a theater genius. I own all of his books, plus books about him, and I recommend that you study him, too. If you are going to read only one of his titles, however, this is the one.

Acting: The First Six Lessons by Richard Boleslavski, Routledge, 2003. Originally published in 1933, this little and deceptively simple book is essential reading. Boleslavski was a close follower of Stanislavsky and was the founder of the American Lab Theatre.

He was a crucial link in the introduction of Stanislavsky's theories in the U.S.

The Audition Book: Winning Strategies for Breaking into Theater, Film, and TV (revised third edition) by Ed Hooks, Back Stage Books, 2000. Yes, this is my own book, and yes I consider it to be essential reading. I won't be so immodest to put the rest of my titles on the essential list, but this one is special. In it, I explain the differences between auditions for stage, film, TV, commercials, and so on. It's good solid information, which is why it is now in its third edition. Go to my Web site www.edhooks.com for references to my other books.

Playing Shakespeare: An Actor's Guide by John Barton, Anchor Press, 2001. This book was a companion to the 1980 BBC TV series of the same name. Copies of the series itself are really hard to find but are worth the effort. The greatest actors from the Royal Shakespeare Company participated in an invaluable study of what it means to act Shakespeare. Even without seeing the series, the book is fabulous. If you have this plus a copy of the series, you have a treasure.

Actors on Acting: The Theories, Techniques, and Practices of the World's Great Actors, Told in Their Own Words, edited by Toby Cole and Helen Krich Chinoy, Three Rivers Press, 1995. I have owned at least six copies of this classic over the years. It is one of those books it is best not to loan out. You won't read it in one sitting because it is more like a mini-encyclopedia than a straightforward acting book. It is an essential addition to your library.

Respect for Acting by Uta Hagen, John Wiley & Sons, 1973. Ms. Hagen, who died in 2004, was one of the great acting teachers. Her influence on me is tangible. This is an excellent how-to acting book.

A Challenge for the Actor by Uta Hagen, Scribner, 1991. This book is really an extension of her earlier one, *Respect for Acting*. Read them in that order.

Secrets of Screen Acting (second edition) by Patrick Tucker, Theatre Arts Books, 2003. I've read a lot of books about acting for film. This one is the best by a good distance. Easy to read, well illustrated, humorous. Tucker is British which also helps. As he points out, a disproportionate number of British actors have excelled in movies. It probably is because they have a tendency to think like he does in this book.

RECOMMENDED READING

Eleanora Duse by Helen Sheehy, Alfred Knopf, 2003. Duse was an early and important inspiration to Stanislavsky. She was self-taught and is generally considered to be the first modern actress.

A Dream of Passion: The Development of the Method by Lee Strasberg, New American Library, 1990. You've heard of Method acting, yes? Well that is really Strasberg's Method, which is derived from Stanislavsky's system. In this book, the renowned teacher explains the basics of the Method.

An Actor Prepares by Constantin Stanislavsky, Theatre Arts Books, 2002. This is the first of the great teacher's books. It is written as a kind of diary of a theater company. In it, he presents the basic ideas of his system.

Building a Character by Constantin Stanislavsky, Theatre Arts Books, 2002. The second of Stanislavsky's books. Be sure to read *An Actor Prepares* first.

Creating a Role by Constantin Stanislavsky, Theatre Arts Books, 2002. This is the third and final of Stanislavsky's trilogy.

A Practical Handbook for the Actor by Melissa Bruder, Vintage, 1986. This slim actor-friendly book was written by several actors who have all worked closely with playwright David Mamet in Chicago. Easy to read and very useful.

Tragedy and Comedy by Walter Kerr, Simon & Shuster, 1968. This title is unfortunately out of print but you can still find copies of it for under $10 online. Walter Kerr was a brilliant observer and critic of theater and his take on comedy and tragedy is priceless. If this book were in print, I would have it on my essential reading list.

Artaud for Beginners by Gabriela Stoppelman, Writers and Readers, 2000. Antonin Artaud is a very important figure in the evolution of modern acting theory, but he can be difficult to read. Therefore, I recommend that you pick up this book when you also purchase *The Theatre and Its Double* by Artaud.

The Theatre and Its Double by Antonin Artaud, Grove Press, 1988. This book was first published back in the 1930s and is still important. In it, Artaud presents his ideas about what he calls "the theatre of cruelty." It is fascinating reading that delves into Jungian psychology and challenges some of the basic concepts of Western theater.

Towards a Poor Theatre by Jerzy Growtowski, Routledge, 2002. Growtowski is not subway reading but he is important. Among his many admirers is Peter Brook, who wrote the intoduction to this book. Growtowski advocated an extremely physical approach to theater and to acting, and his ideas have influenced many acting teachers, including me.

A Life by Elia Kazan, DaCapo Press, 1997. This is maybe the best theatrical autobiography I have ever read. Kazan was the director of choice for Broadway shows in the 1950s. He discovered Marlon Brando, James Dean, Warren Beatty, and others. He was a founding member of the famous Actors Studio and directed most of the great plays by Tennessee Williams, Arthur Miller, and William Inge, as well as the movie *On the Waterfront*. His perspective on what makes a good film actor is invaluable, and his life (he died in 2003) was extraordinary and controversial.

On Directing by Harold Clurman, Touchstone Books, 1997. Clurman was a founding member of the Group Theatre in New York. He was there when Strasberg's Method acting was formulated. This book is a terrific history of the period as well as a very practical guide. It probably should be on my list of essential reading. Close call.

The Fervent Years: The Group Theatre in the Thirties by Harold Clurman, DaCapo Press, 1988. This is the best book I have read about the evolution of the Group Theatre. If you are a beginning actor, you should definitely read it. This is your heritage.

The Presence of the Actor by Joseph Chaikin, Macmillan, 1973. Joe Chaikin was one of the most important theorists to come out of the 1960s experimental theater scene. He began with the Living Theatre in the 1950s and then was a director with the Open Theatre in the 1960s. This is not a how-to book. It is a perspective on theater, acting, the audience, and the world. I pull this one off the shelf and re-read it from time to time and I always get something good from it.

Acting in Film: An Actor's Take on Movie Making by Michael Caine, Applause Books, 2000. Michael Caine is a consummate film actor, and he generously shares some of his secrets in this book. There is also a videotape that goes with the book if you can find it. Quite excellent.

The Working Actor's Toolkit by Jean Schiffman, Heinemann, 2003. Ms. Schiffman is a long-time personal friend of mine and I am happy to recommend her book. What she did was go around and talk to umpteen acting teachers about thorny acting problems, like playing drunk or playing crazy. I'm quoted in there of course. Jean, a former actor herself, has been a regular columnist for *Back Stage West* newspaper.

The Lord of the Rings: Gollum—How We Made Movie Magic by Andy Serkis, Houghton Mifflin, 2003. Gollum is an all-digital character that was created by a live actor in collaboration with skilled animators at WETA Digital in New Zealand for the *Lord of the Rings* film trilogy. In the future there will be more of such animated characters, and it is a good idea for you to understand something about the process. Andy Serkis, the actor who was behind Gollum, wrote this wonderful book, which is very actor-to-actor in tone. When he began working on *The Lord of the Rings* he was already a highly trained and experienced actor but he knew nothing at all about animation. This is essentially a diary of his journey to animated stardom. Excellent book. I was truly enraptured with it.

The Way of the Actor: A Path to Knowledge and Power by Brian Bates, Shambhala, 2001. Actors are shamans. Brian Bates is a psychologist who has studied the psychology of acting and has taught at the Royal Academy of Dramatic Art in London. This is one of the few contemporary and available books that address the shamanistic roots of acting.

Index

About the Author

Ed Hooks is a member of all performing unions and has been a professional actor for over thirty years. His extensive acting credits span all media and include many stage plays, more than 150 television commercials, and upwards of 100 television shows. He received his initial training as an actor in New York, where he lived and worked for nine years. He spent thirteen years in Hollywood, twelve years in San Francisco, and currently lives in Chicago. Ed has been teaching his highly regarded professional-level acting classes for more than twenty years, and many of his students are working actors today.

In addition to teaching acting to actors, Ed is one of the few people in the world who teach acting to animators. Wearing this hat, he has taught for many major companies, including Walt Disney Animation, Lucas Arts, Pacific Data Images, Electronic Arts, BioWare, Valve Software, and Midway Games. He has taught acting for animators for several years at Filmakademie Baden-Württemburg in Ludwigsberg, Germany, and has been a featured speaker at various animation festivals, including Animex in Teesside, England, and FMX in Stuttgart, Germany. His book *Acting for Animators* is required reading at many top animation schools.

Ed is also the author of two other books published by Watson-Guptill: *The Audition Book: Winning Strategies for Breaking into Theater, Film, and Television* (third edition, revised) and *The Ultimate Scene and Monologue Sourcebook*. You can get a larger overview of Ed's work, plus a detailed resume, by visiting his Web sites, www.edhooks.com and www.ActingForAnimators.com.